VOICES WITHIN A TEENAGE MIND

JOSH D. MORTON

KITSAP PUBLISHING

Voices Within a Teenage Mind
Second edition, published 2017

By Josh D. Morton
Illustrations by Shelly Kay

Copyright © 2017, Josh Morton

ISBN-13: 978-1-942661-72-6

All rights reserved. No part of this book may be reproduced or transmitted in any form or by any means, electronic or mechanical, including photocopying, recording or by any information storage and retrieval system, without written permission from the author, except for the inclusion of brief quotations in a review.

Published by Kitsap Publishing
P.O. Box 572
Poulsbo, WA 98370
www.KitsapPublishing.com

Printed in the United States of America

TD 20170801

100-10 9 8 7 6 5 4 3 2 1

CONTENTS

Foreword "Voices Within A Teenage Mind"	I
A Dysfunctional Upbringing	1
Individuality	19
Life in Poverty	29
Alone	33
Death	45
Faith	55
A Shaped Environment	61
Divorce/Absentia	77
The Negative Influences of Others	93
Insecurity/Self-Image	107
What's Important	127

** As you navigate through this book you will find some names with two asterisks. These are new entries to our 2017 edition! We wanted to make sifting through this book easier for those that read our 2016 edition.

FOREWORD "VOICES WITHIN A TEENAGE MIND"

By Josh D. Morton

June 14, 2017

Teaching Language Arts to 7th and 8th graders for the past 14 years has been an incredibly rewarding job. I always laugh when people say, "You're a brave soul" or, "I don't know how you do it", for I feel neither statement at all. Early in my teaching career, my father gave me a copy of the book <u>Teaching with Fire</u>. This book of poems shows the drive and passion of teachers and it unexpectedly impacted me. Now that I'm a veteran teacher, I realize it's not about my passion so much as getting the passion out of my students. I started thinking, "Where is their forum to voice what drives them, or doesn't?"

The 8th grade classroom feels like home to me, and for an hour a day, each young teenager is there to learn about the world and himself/herself. While I pride myself on teaching them how to construct a well-thought-out essay, or aspire for kids to think critically about literature presented to them, I also love the challenge of showing them the world they come from and the relevance of it to what they are learning because it is essential for them to seek independence, confidence, motivation, and most importantly, their identities. We always finish the school year reading S.E. Hinton's <u>The Outsiders</u>, which seems to be one of the few books most of my students' parents have read as well, thus allowing for family conversation.

The last essay of the year that they write consists of two prompts: First, they discuss people and events that have shaped who they are today, and the second part of the essay asks them to gauge how much of their "true self" comes into play with various groups of people. Does their true identity shine at home with a sibling or parent, or at school with a best friend or group of friends? I sat in disbelief when I read their eye-opening responses. It's easy to teach with blinders on, knowing on the surface many students are emotionally and/or physically bruised. All these years I have been telling them to keep focusing on their studies because education will set them free. After reading their essays (which really read like memoirs), I realized they had stories to share with the world. It's easy to talk about broken systems in education, parenting, and government, but when reading the following memoirs and the ups and downs of these kids, I can only think of the tough life many of them have lived, and the broken hearts that accompany them. Keep in mind, these are personal stories the kids have kept close to the vest, because kids in general bury their emotions and put on a brave front. These are their stories, with the stipulation their names be changed to protect their identities. I have omitted my judgments, to let you come up with your own conclusions about the voices within a teenage mind.

We wear the mask that grins and lies,
It hides our cheeks and shades our eyes,--
This debt we pay to human guile;
With torn and bleeding hearts we smile,
And mouth with myriad subtleties.

Why should the world be overwise,
In counting all our tears and sighs?
Nay, let them only see us, while
We wear the mask.

We smile, but, O great Christ, our cries
To thee from tortured souls arise.
We sing, but oh the clay is vile
Beneath our feet, and long the mile;
But let the world dream otherwise,
We wear the mask!

--Paul Laurence Dunbar

To my dad, who said I'd be published someday.
To my mom for giving me a love of words
To my sister for helping shape who I have become
To my wife, Kolleen, and children Riley, Tyler, Madison, and Alex. You are my inspiration.

CHAPTER 1

A DYSFUNCTIONAL UPBRINGING

JACKIE, 14

About two years ago in the summer, my mom told me that she wasn't my mom. I didn't understand what she meant when she explained it, like maybe I was adopted. She explained that she was really my grandma and that my "sister" was my real mom. She told me she wanted to tell me when I was younger, but didn't want me hating her. I was totally shocked. I found out that I have five brothers and sisters. I used to go to school and church with them before I knew. My "baby brother" was actually adopted by a lady that's friends with my mom. My other brothers and sister doesn't talk to me anymore. This impacted me for the good in that my grandma raised me well, and that it doesn't matter who your mom is. I am actually pretty happy that my "grandma" is my mom. She is a big part of my life and she helps me learn right from wrong. She is my role model, and I am thankful to have a mom that makes me a better person. It also makes my life better knowing that she'll always think of me as her daughter.

**LAYLA, 14

I have lived in poverty all my life. I was obviously a mistake of irresponsible drinking when my mom was 18 and my dad was 22, and my dad spent over half of my life in jail. I could never go and see him, and just when I started to see him after he finished his sentence, he ran into trouble again and spent another four years in jail. My mom was a drunk from my birth to when I was around eight years old. She has since gotten the help she needed, but at the time she was drinking, I experienced multiple pull-overs by the police and a couple of car accidents. My mother dated a lot of losers who were either rude or abusive to her. One of her boyfriends, my dad's brother, was high on meth and drunk and decided it was a good idea to go ride his dirt bike on the train tracks at 3 a.m. He flipped his dirt bike 100 feet and went flying, breaking his back in several places. He was found half alive four hours later, but paralyzed for life. When he was taken to the hospital, my mom would spend days with him in the hospital, while I stayed home alone and isolated in our tiny house. After three months of this crap, he was finally released and my mom in her ever flowing wisdom thought it would be a good idea to live in his garage. We lived there for six months, with my mom loyally helping him and dedicating all her time with him. We bolted after he started to get rude to her and we finally got another home. It was nice to finally be somewhere comforting. About 3 months of being single, she met this nice guy named Jarrett, who has Multiple Sclerosis. Three months later they found a big house for us and his one-year old daughter. After seven months of pretty happy times, of course, things got a little twisted. Mom and Jarrett started fighting, which messed me and my step-sister up. A few months later, my mom and I moved out into the place we live in now, but it was really hard to leave my step-sister. I think we've finally found our happiness. We live in a 3-bedroom house on 20 acres, with animals everywhere, and we were happy! After about a month of living here my life changed for the better when my grandma moved in with us. When she first moved in, I was always testing her, talking back, and saying stupid things because I was a real brat back then. Grams changed every little thing about me, emotionally, mentally, and physically. She taught me the importance of life, and all the downsides of life, and how twisted it can be. She taught me how to ride her mustang horse, Casper, who is my best friend to this day. But, knowing my life, all good things seem to come to abrupt ends. Grams and Mom started fighting because my mom was jealous of all the time I was spending with Grams. She called me into her room one day, when I entered, she was teary eyed. She asked me to sit down, and she told me about her life. She told me all about the darkness that life has shown her. She told me about her heartbreaks, her parents, her supernatural sense, her best friend who was killed in a car accident, in which Grams predicted before it even happened. She told me about traveling the world, and how she met all three of her husbands. She told me she was thrown out of a car, had to live as a prostitute for years to survive, and had six abortions. She told me about being raped and impregnated at 13 years old. Oh, and she had been announced dead twice from drug overdoses. But then her tone changed when she told me about the beauty that life can bring. She told me about how animals comforted her in hard situations, how much she loves her three children, how heavenly it feels to ride a horse with her arms out, and how the rest of the world disappears while doing so. She slipped back into the dark side after a while. She told me about how her parents never talked to her or taught her the right way by talking it through, and instead they would just whack her hands with a metal ruler. She was always in her room, trying to avoid them, so she retreated into books because she didn't have anything else to do. She ran away from home at 14 and met drugs. At this point she stopped talking and was sobbing. I was crying too. It hit me so hard. It made me so thankful for the things I had, helped me love my mom again, made me feel different, and we became super close after that. My mom and Grams continued to fight though. Mom was like an abusive husband, and Grams was like an enslaved wife, but, when Grams dragged her to a counselor's office and explained everything, my mom twisted everything around and my grandma was diagnosed as having mental health issues. Yes,

Grams definitely has mental problems, but Mom just took advantage of that fact

I had a tough 7th grade between drama, fistfights, and friends moving away.

Grams got in serious enough trouble that the police were involved and she was forced to move out a month later. She moved into a place where tweakers lived. She was doing meth and heroin, and wasn't taking care of her animals. After a health scare, she decided to get clean of all drugs, and moved back to my house and is 8 months sober today.

There's no denying my Grams has played a big part of my life. Without her, I believe I would be a troubled teen, doing drugs, or even dead. It's unconventional the ways I've learned lessons but all of them have helped shape me. I've learned that drugs screw up lives, and I will never do them. I've learned that there are definitely harder lives out there in the world, and I am thankful for what I have. I learned a lot about animals. I learned how to deal with my anger, and how to deal with school; bullies especially. I learned, this year, that I have to accept things that I can't control, and letting go of those situations. I learned that anger, has no point. It doesn't fix anything, it just makes it worse. I learned that boys are dumb and I will live in a big mansion, which I will afford, because I will be successful, surrounded by my animals. I also learned that love is very powerful and difficult thing, and sometimes hard to handle.

PRESLEY, 14

I have a book. A simple composition a book. A book no one knows about and no one ever will. I can be myself. I can say how I feel and I can extrapolate my feelings. I love writing because I'm full and empty of absolutely everything all at once. Is trusting someone even possible?

It seems as if when you tell your closest friend something, she tells her closest friend, and that friend tells her closest friend and soon everyone knows. The feeling of not always having someone makes you feel so weak and hopeless. I can't rely on anyone.

In the 6th grade my teacher required me to write a poem. A poem about the world starting with "Inside this..." and this is what I wrote:

Inside this world that we live in I've come to realize it's full of sin. There is no escaping where we are, no matter what we do or who we are. There is yelling, screaming, violence, and pain, but one day it will go away. There's moaning, crying, but it's all the same because most people don't care anyway. I guess I'm like a book, but I don't want to be read because I'm scared about what these people have said. Is it all truth? Is it all a lie? Do we still deserve to live our lives? I don't know and I shouldn't care, but I should know that life isn't fair.

Ever since then I've been writing. It has taught me so much about myself I never knew. I will write until I can't keep my eyes open anymore at night. It's the one thing that makes me feel better. It's the one thing that I can turn to and the one thing I can trust not to change upon me. Writing does not change; the author does. A few summers ago, my mom went absolutely insane. Prescribed medications made her crazy to the point I was convinced the devil was on her side. She was convinced that I was a demon possessed creature. She also believed that my dad was watching her through her phone camera, the PlayStation camera, and every colored blinking light in the house. She also thought my dad hired 3,200 Mexicans to watch every move and track her car's location. I started second-guessing my dad and believing everything she'd ever said to me, because when you love a person so much you feel bad not believing something they say no matter how crazy it sounds. For about two years she lived in her parents' yard in a small little trailer about 6 feet wide and 14 ft long and for about a year that was where I spent a lot of my time. There was a time when I wasn't able to see her because authorities were worried about what was she was going to do next. She was unpredictable not in a dangerous way, but they thought it was better that we didn't have contact. After about 8 months of not being able to see or hear from her, I remember hearing her voice. My heart sort of fell. I felt abandoned, but I knew it wasn't her choice to cut contact with me. My dad wasn't in the best place either, dealing with alcohol issues. He was trying to do as much as he could to get rid of the pain he was feeling by drinking and smoking. He didn't do that in front of me and my little brother, but I knew. He said he doesn't want us going down the same roads, but doesn't model it. I wasn't only "mom" to my little brother, but I had to be "dad" and "sister" to him as well, especially when my dad left for Alaska for work.

While he was gone, I suspected my mom was cheating on my dad with a neighbor thought I trusted. My dad didn't believe me for a while, but then he pulled me in my room for a rare heart-to-heart conversation. He said. "Presley, you were right. Mom has been sleeping with Sam." I never wanted to believe anything I thought, but I started crying and my head filled with so many questions and thoughts. So many angry emotions. Usually you wouldn't want to hear something like that, but I was so happy that I did. I always felt disconnected from my father, but that night was the only night I ever saw my dad cry. That night I also received one of only four hugs over the last four years; and one of the two "I love yous" I ever heard.

LAINEY, 14

When you grow up, you remember the big things, not the little things. In my family, mental illnesses are the little things, and how we act out are the big things. My dad's bipolar and he acts out a lot, which means a lot of yelling.

Growing up with a bipolar dad makes the house more like hell. I have memories of my dad yelling and screaming at us, and him kicking my mom out of the house and the car. It happened seven times in less than a year when I was eight years old. We were homeless and living in whichever house would allow us to.

I remember one time when I was five years old and living with my uncle and my dad screamed at my mom, saying, "you're not a mom, just leave, get out and never come back." Once she left, he had other women come over. The problem left for a year or two, but it came back last year and it's just been getting worse since then. He would randomly just blow up on us. See, we don't have a lot of money, and yesterday, my mom bought two bags of chips because I was hungry, and he started screaming at me: telling me I should have gotten up earlier to eat and that now he won't be able to afford his derby parts and gas. He also told me to get over myself and grow a pair because I started crying. This happens more than anyone thinks. When he starts to yell at me or anyone else, I either yell back because I, myself, am bipolar, or I have a panic attack because of anxiety.

I wish my dad knew how not to yell, but he doesn't. I wish we had more money, but we don't. I wish I didn't have anxiety or Bipolar Disorder, but I do. I wish I was numb to my dad yelling at me, but I'm not. And sometimes-just sometimes-I wish he would leave and never come back.

ANNIE, 14

I have always grown up in a dysfunctional/emotional family. It has made me realize who I want to be and who I know I DON'T want to be. My mom and dad split when I was just a baby. They both had no idea how they wanted to live their lives. They still don't. My mom was a meth addict for as long as I can remember. I lived for years not knowing this until I was old enough to notice how she picked at her face, and how she would stay up all night and never sit down to relax, or she would sleep three days straight and never show an appetite. My dad is the same way. I know he stays up all night, even though I never see him. My aunt and uncle do hardcore drugs too. They like snorting cocaine or shooting up heroin. None of them have careers. How could they? I wanna be successful. I don't wanna be an addict with no life, so I surround myself with people who want to be successful and have a life. Despite what I know I want, I can only be myself with one person. She has gone through the same thing as me. I'm not fake around my friends, just guarded. I don't tell everybody else about my life or what happened to me because I don't want my friends to feel bad for me, and I don't want them to ask me a million questions. I just wanna be happy when I am not home. I'm also guarded at school because people judge me and spread rumors about me. Most of the time I don't let it get to me, but sometimes I enter a depression and don't even know it. I can't concentrate on school work and I become quieter. When I am home, I prefer being in solitude unless I have friends over. That's when I want to be outside the whole entire time or be anywhere besides home, because I think it's embarrassing my family has messed up their life.

CONSTANCE, 14

For as far back as I can remember my parents were never really stable. I would go to sleep at night not knowing whether or not my mom or dad would be there when I woke up. My mom and dad would fight at least three times a week. It would get so bad to where I had to take my little brother outside or to the very back room of the house and distract him. Now me being almost 3 and my brother being about 2 we never fully understood what was going on, but it was still hard on us. I have lived with my grandparents since the day I was born and still live with them today. My mom was shoved into "adulthood" at a young age since she had me at 19 years old. Sadly, she never really took action of that adulthood till 13 years after I was born.

When I was 4 my mom kicked my dad out for the first time. She eventually got a boyfriend named Luther. My mom, Luther, my brother, and I all lived together in a tiny 2 bedroom apartment. I can't really remember Luther but I used to trust him, sadly. One day my mom and he got into an argument and he beat her up pretty bad. My brother and I were in the room watching the whole time and we couldn't do anything about it since we were so little. I remember he had her pinned to the bed and the only thing I could think of doing was hitting him with a pillow, but it did no good. Eventually he left and my mom called the cops and my grandparents, who got a flight to California from Alaska overnight. The cops came and they took me and my brother to a children's home. We weren't in there long and my grandparents came and got us after about 3 days. My mom left Luther and eventually got back with my dad, but that wasn't the last time something like this would happen.

When I was 9 my grandparents were still with us and we lived in a beautiful home in Corona, California. My mom kicked my dad out multiple times before we moved here, and did it for what she thought was the last time when we moved in here. He only came to visit maybe twice a year. My mom had three boyfriends over this time span of three years. Jerry was her first boyfriend. They were old high school friends and for some reason my mom decided to go live in Alaska with him. He was never home, instead at bars and clubs while my mom stayed home. She eventually had an abortion, due to the baby dying before it was developed. We lived up there for nine months before everything fell apart and we moved back in with my grandparents. My mom fell into a dark spiral of bad choices and trouble.

She got a new boyfriend named Steven who was the first person to introduce her to drugs and stealing. At first I didn't notice it, eventually she was never home and I started to get more worried. She was put on trial for stealing a camera, that she didn't take, but since they found her with some drugs, they just put her on house arrest with an ankle monitor. Eventually they broke up and Steven kind of became a stalker, but ended up in trouble with the cops and moved away.

Then there was Chuck. Chuck was the worst boyfriend she had. He was an alcoholic himself and helped my mom get more drugs. She never came home and my grandma worked from home raising my brother who was 9. My sister who was 5, and I. I was only 11 and knowing your mom was off doing drugs and other illegal things hits you hard at that age. Eventually Chuck and my mom broke up and he went crazy. I remember waking up to my mom crying and my grandpa on the phone with the cops. Chuck was threatening to hurt my family and was banging on the windows of our house. We called the cops and the went around checking our house and making sure everything was clear before leaving and we never heard from him again.

A few months later I came home from school to my grandma telling me my mom won't be home for a while because the cops came to do a drug check on her, since she had an ankle monitor, and found cocaine. When she first told me I was madder at my mom than anything. I thought she was finally getting better and was pulling herself together. Later that night at 11:34 p.m. my grandma woke me up saying my mom was on the phone. I talked to her for two minutes before I broke down crying and gave the phone back to my grandma. All the anger in me disappeared and I was just so broken on why this was happening to my family. My dad bailed my mom out of jail that night and they were home around noon the next day. I didn't know if I felt closer or more distant to my mom after that, but I felt a little tense around her for a while. One day she was going to take me to a store, where she was going to pick up drugs I didn't know about, but we got into a car accident before we were even close to the store. We hit a parked truck and moved it at least 40 feet into the next yard. The car was completely totaled, and my mom hit the windshield, cutting her head open pretty badly. I was bent down, but I was really lucky and only had a minor cut on my shin. About 6 months later, my dad moved back in and we all we moved to Port Orchard to get my mom out of California and start a new life style.

Going through all these things at such a young age forced me to mature faster from the beginning. I've lived a lot of teenage mistakes through my mom and know where things can take me in life if I make the wrong choice. I've learned that alcohol leads to hardships and addiction and drugs lead to near death. My mom has made positive changes in these past two years and is now a nursing assistant near my school. I know kids my age usually don't see the full effect of these things and only hear about them, but I feel like me seeing them first hand was a good life lesson for me even if it made my life more difficult. I still live with my grandparents and my parents still have a hard time with money and other things, but overall I couldn't have asked for a better life. I love my family and I'm so proud of my mom for how far she's come and grateful for all the things she's taught me in life.

RICK, 14

My grandpa was the first one to hold me when I was born. It was a very happy day for my family--one of the few. My half-sister didn't like me one bit growing up. She thought I was stealing her light and she didn't like that. She held a grudge against me from the moment she knew I existed. She would often propose putting me up for adoption. I grew up in a neighborhood that had many people--almost none of them good. It's not what my parents wanted, but it's what we could afford, and as long as we had a roof over our head and food on our plates, along with water in our glasses, we were good. I remember many arguments between my mom and dad, most of them caused by my mother. At the age of five my mom and dad divorced and I went with my mom to an apartment for about two years, until we moved right next to my now-best friend. I would crawl under the fence and be at his house! It was a lot of fun for three years, and then we moved out of the rental and into our current home. Around the time we moved into that house, my mother was diagnosed bipolar, but she refused to be put on medication or therapy. This has hurt me and my step-dad-who has been with us since I was seven years old-because we are the ones who have taken on her anger. Though it's only words, those words have slowly killed my step-dad and me. First, it was happening at least once a night, and it was very rare to go one or two nights without an argument. About a year later the screaming calmed just enough to narrow down to four arguments a week, which still sucked. On the social side of life, I was about twelve when my best friend from kindergarten moved and said he hated me. I took it as a joke, but it really hurt. It was a lot to take in between that, my mom calling me "retarded" when she got angry (and saying she meant it), and my dad being gone on mandatory business trips. The only people I felt I could be myself with were my friends and my grandparents, so I started spending a lot of time with them because they were there for me, and that way I could get away from my mom and cool down for a little while. I started to be much happier and everything around me seemed better. But when 7th grade came along I started hanging out with some people that treated me like crap and only let me hang out with them so they could have someone to make jokes about and tease. There was one person in the group that didn't like it, but she didn't do anything, and I acted like the "jokes" didn't hurt. They did. Depression started setting in, yet I hid it really well. I really wasn't okay. I tried to commit suicide, but thankfully, my best friend since the 3rd grade stopped me. To regulate my emotions, I started going outside more and riding my bike for exercise, and I felt a lot happier going into 8th grade. But my mom's yelling reached all-time low, and I felt trapped living with her. I became a recluse and I didn't want to go outside. My friends forced me outside, and it's helped, but I am making efforts to move out of my mom's house and into my dad's because it is a better environment for me, and I am a lot happier at my dad's. Despite growing up in an environment of poverty and mental illness, I am proud of myself for pulling myself out of a hole. I would say I am at a high point in my life. I just hope that point keeps going higher.

MINNA, 13

I live with my grandparents-who love my three brothers and me-because when I was four my mom decided to give me up. She asked her friend to take care of me but was denied, so she called the cops to put me in foster care. When I heard the knock on the door, I retreated under my mom's bed, knowing who it was. Not having a rebellious trait in my body, I went out when a man asked where I was. I remember it like a dream-some parts I remember and some parts I don't. It was dark outside and a blonde lady bent down towards me. She asked me if I wanted to stay with my two brothers or be split apart. My brothers annoyed me, but I loved them. I replied that I wanted to stay together. We bounced around from foster care home to foster care home. Sometimes we were apart, sometimes not. I don't even think my other brother was alive. I remember the first foster home, we were in, my brother was sitting in my pink Cinderella chair so I pushed him and he fell back into a glass coffee table and broke it.

At the age of five my grandparents took me in, but after a few months my dad wanted me. At his house he had a wife and my two other brothers. After his wife got bored of dressing me up like a pretty doll, she didn't love me anymore. She bought toys for my brothers, and when she got home from shopping I asked her why I never got anything. She said it was because I wet the bed. I was only seven, I couldn't help it. I did wet the bed a lot, so I got spanked a lot, even in front of my friends. I'd rather not share my embarrassing and repulsive things she did to me. I tried to leave by telling my mom on a visit, a lie, that she spanked me with the metal end of the belt. My mom called somebody, but it didn't work, I dreaded what was going to happen to me when I got home. Luckily, when I got home I never got punished because my dad was there. A couple months later I moved back to my grandparents' home. It was Valentine's Day and my sister, who never felt the negative side of my dad's ex-wife out of the WHOLE family, was talking to her and asked me if I wanted to talk to my mom. Of course I didn't have any sense to deny it as an 8-year-old. I always did what people asked me. She handed me the phone and I said "hi" very shyly. She said in an unfriendly tone, "Why are you pouting?" I busted out crying, "How could she say that?"

    I didn't have any hatred towards her; I still don't. I saw her one time a few years ago and waved and she just glared at me. I guess I was crying because I knew would never have a mom that'll love me. If I ever saw her again, I would put on a smile and hold back the tears. My grandparents decided to adopt my brothers and me in 2006. Everything started being normal. I stopped being depressed about having no mom. I just realized I'd never see her again. I know I can see her when I turn 18, but if your mom doesn't love you now, she'll never love you. In second grade I met my best and only friend. I stuck to her like glue until seventh grade. If you could find my best friend, you could find me. Our bond felt unbreakable. But, in sixth grade I noticed she was pushing me away, so I cried myself to sleep every night, clutching the heart she gave me in third grade that signified friendship forever. In seventh grade, she gave me a forgiveness card, apologizing for ignoring me. Though I started crying instantly, I knew we would never have that bond again simply because we're just too different. In seventh grade, I felt like I had no friends. I focused on school and went to the library when I had no one to hang out with, and tried to forget about the pain. Fortunately, I have friends now and grandparents who love me. I would say I have your average teenage problems. My past is still an open wound, but as long as I don't talk or think about it, I won't cry. I'm my own person, and if something's pulling me down I'll make it stop because I refuse to have those problems anymore.

JIMMER, 14

Many people look at me and judge who I am, without knowing my life and what I have gone through. You see, many people think I have no problems in life because my family has money. Boy can I tell you that those people are wrong. My mom was a drug user and was in and out of jail. How do you tell a two-year-old his mom won't come home in years? Drugs drove my parents apart. My mother thought it was my fault that her life was screwed up. She would come home drugged up and beat me until she heard my dad's car pull up. She used to pick me up by the ears and scream in my face. She would wrap cords around the doors so that I could not get out, then she would leave me there for hours until my father came home. How does someone beat a 4-year-old? How does a mother beat her only child? This started fights between my parents. My mom got picked up for an armed robbery and my problems amplified 10 times worse. My dad had to raise me and my step-brother as a single parent, but when I was five years old he met this girl named Kira. Life seemed easier at that point in life. We did so many things as a family. We would go out to eat, have vacations and play card games. But, like everything else in my life, things started to deteriorate. Now my step-mother, Kira showed hatred towards my step-brother to the point that he had to go live with my grandma. My step-mom became meaner and meaner. I was so tired from it that I stayed at friends' houses as much as possible to get away from her. She would make me do chores for hours and tell me everything that I do is wrong. This went on for many years. Only recently, in my early teen years, has she become willing to work on our relationship. My life might not be the best, but it has taught me that you can only trust a few people that are close to you, that you can recover from things that are bad, and that anyone can change. It's also important to not judge people, because you never know the things that happen to them behind closed doors.

CHAPTER 2

INDIVIDUALITY

SALENE, 14

Everyone I know seems to have some sort of sob story (especially my friends). Not that there is anything wrong with that, but it's just the way it is. I, however, do not have what most people would call a "hard life". For the majority of people, my life is perfect. To them, I have good grades, lots of friends, nice parents, and very good health. But that's just the outside. Even when people know what my life is like, it still doesn't seem that bad. My closest friends still think it's better than theirs. My biological parents are no longer together (they never married and broke up before I was born, and now I live with my mom and sadly am still forced to see my dad). My six-year-old brother has been wearing dresses to the point where my strictly religious grandparents are not welcoming him into their home if he is to be himself in that way. Like most teenagers, I have my own insecurities and fight with my mom more often than before. I credit my individuality for creating the person I am today. Yes, I know, everyone is unique and special in his or her own way or whatever they're talking about those Disney princess movies. That's not what I mean though. I'm talking about how you put me in a room with a group of people and I am the friendliest, most outgoing, talkative, loud, sarcastic, weirdest person you'll ever meet. I embarrass myself so much that I hardly notice anymore. But out of nowhere I can become very angry and defensive. At times it can be kind of funny, but most of the time my friends have to try and get me to calm down. Having such a loud mouth gets me into lots of trouble, which is not too fun. At my school along with any other place in the world, there are little groups of people that have very similar personalities, yet I am not one of those people who easily fits in with people who are just like me, because there is no one like me! My friends are my friends because they are the only people that come close to understanding me. But I guess they didn't ALWAYS have my back. In elementary school I was dragged into a lot of drama-many times alone-with people who didn't like me and wanted to make a big deal out of it. At the time I didn't know what to do, so I went along with it, and man was that a bad idea. I spent all my time with these people who I thought were my friends, and I put up with all of their crap because I thought I would be a bad person if I didn't. Yet they just slowly dragged me down farther and farther away from reality, until I was alone. As I got older I started to become friends with better people, and I realized how stupid all the drama was and how to avoid it. I got into basketball and started focusing on my acting. As a result I became tougher and started standing up more for myself and others. Everything seemed to be going really well. That is until recently, when I started fighting with both my biological parents (and my step-mom) more. What was really sad about that, however, is that my step dad (who is more of a father than my "real dad" will ever be) stopped taking my side, and I became more upset on the inside. All these fights have slowly torn me apart. I love my mom and we used to get along so well, but all of a sudden everything between us broke. Not only that, but now I am secretly very insecure about myself and am no longer able to truthfully say a lot of good things about me. I have developed a habit, without knowing, of always trying to look happy because as soon as I drop my smile or my attitude changes I know people will realize something is up and they will ask me about it. Compared to my friends, I may be an alien, but luckily they care for me just the same. I may not have one story that, if I were to tell someone, they would feel really bad for me and say they're sorry for no reason, but I do have over 14 years of small life-changing events that have made me smarter with the choices I make; humorous with the jokes I say; braver because I have the courage to do what's right; protective of myself and others; stronger because I have been through pain; and kinder, for no one deserves to suffer. Each of these traits are parts of who I am and that's what makes me different: You will never find another soul like mine. It makes me feel special to be one of a kind.

MILLA, 14

I honestly don't think humans were created to be happy with their identity. If someone says they are, they're either a narcissist or a liar. Really, no matter how you look at it, humanity is constantly growing and improving for the better (so it seems). But then we have setbacks like wars, famine and human apathy. You would think when overcoming these things earlier in history, humans would learn and grow from those setbacks. I've concluded the human species is a collection of weeds; a pesky invasive species that just so happens to be beautiful and always taking up more land and destroying more crops. You could say that the goal of humanity itself is forever human innovation. Now, saying this, whose right is it to say they're truly happy with their identity when they can also stand there and name hundreds of things they've never done and never will do, or thousands of things they can never sympathize for and millions of things they'll never know about? It certainly isn't my right. I assume that means I'm not happy with my identity, but I do believe wholeheartedly that I'm improving every day. I don't hate myself, it's more that I hate when I'm not improving myself.

I've come to realize I don't know my "friends" very well. They aren't bad people, but I do think that I don't completely know who they are. Do they know who I am? I don't think so. Learning about people is such a careful and tedious thing. You make a wrong assumption, or say the wrong thing, and they're disgusted that you don't understand them. Maybe it's just me. I don't get people well, but also I'm a fantastic read of character. What a circumstance.

Honestly, I don't really know who I am but I know everything about me. I can speak to how my dad was never around much when I was a kid, or how writing is a way that I cope with bad things and huge ideas. Sometimes if I can find the right word, it makes me feel better. Take sadness for example. Sometimes, when I'm sad--like all teenagers seem to be--I like to refer to it as a pool of water. If I'm upset, I'm drowning. Sometimes when I probably should be upset, but I'm not, I refer to it as a draught. I wonder if people think I'm crazy when they ask about my day and I mumble something about swimming around. I have a writer's mind, perhaps, imaginative and analytic, but also profoundly logical most of the time. Sometimes I can come off as rude, but that's only when I'm trying to problem-solve. Maybe that's why people I try to teach things to always dislike me afterwards.

I can only guess what shaped me into being what I am. I used to think I was born to be well-grounded and book smart over street smart but maybe people aren't just born to be that way. I loved books and learning since I was a young kid, and that smarter logical side of me was developed before I was 5. I always asked questions about everything. Supernovas, dry-docking, economy, law. Oh, especially law. I love the law system. Everyone finds it boring but I think it's one of the most interesting, exquisite things in the world. It's entirely complex and totally human. We made this complicated system of rules and functions and decisions to be the underground leader of our society. I guess that means I'll be in law, journalism, or maybe a digital nomad.

JADE, 14

Some people may view me as an ordinary 14-year-old girl who is like all the other cliché kids out there--a simple teenager that has a bunch of obsessions with celebrities and other things. But, I'm my own person, just like everyone else in the world. For about 10 years of my life, I've been the same, quiet, shy, and bashful girl that I am. But where my personality came from was where I grew up: a small driveway surrounded by trees and many other things that would be outside. I live with both of my parents and we have very few neighbors, and the neighbors we do have are old. Almost no children lived on my street, so I usually spent time with myself, running outside and finding ladybugs. Due to having little interaction with other children, going to school and being stuck with a bunch of kids I didn't know formed my shyness. Although I felt nervous, I had found a friend who eventually became my best friend. By making a new friend, a lot of my nervousness went away. While in preschool, I began to take a liking to drawing because of an online game. I'd draw my character from the game, Princess Ladybug Pinkerhopper. As time went on, I'd make more characters that I came to love. Ever since I learned to read and write, I began writing stories of my dogs doing crazy things. Back when I was six, I wrote a story about my dog, Kandy, sneaking out of the house to go to the dog park and chase cats. My parents always encouraged me to write stories, and would buy me notebooks so I could write as much as I could. Writing was something I'd do once in a while until 4th grade, when my teacher read my story out loud and everyone loved it and was laughing a whole bunch. After finding out I could make people happy just by writing, I began writing nearly every day once my dad bought me Microsoft Word. From writing so much, I'm able to picture anything a little easily. Being able to imagine things, I decided to try getting into 3D animation. Though I'm terrible at animating, I still find it fun and can imagine how the character moves, even if it's not great or accurate. These experiences have helped me develop my love for creativity, which is a daily occurrence now. I'm always too shy to tell anyone about the things I do at home, though. It's like I'm about to tell someone about these things I do, but the words won't come out due to me being too shy, the other person will never stop talking, or they have no interest, so I'm not exactly me when I talk to other people. I'm actually a lot noisier and hyper at home than out in public. But I've been improving and trying to talk more and let my true self come out. I have dreams to show the world myself and to share all my art. In order to make my dreams come true, I've been trying to push away the shyness little by little, even if I don't want to. I hope that they do come true.

HEATHER, 14

Luckily, I'm a part of a family that has not split apart. I am a very sensitive person and because of that, I have a need to open up to people. I know I can count on my mom, and I have amazing friends that I know I can trust with anything. I don't have that many, but the numbers don't count.

As a kid, I learned lessons the tough way--getting spanked. No matter how much I hated it, I know now that teaches you not to do it again. My parents raised me into the person I am today. I'm happy, cheerful, and full of joy, but everyone has that time when they just can't do it anymore. And it seems to be a lot more lately. I don't mean suicidal in any way, I just mean anger and guilt and sadness building up inside to a point where you just can't take it anymore and it comes out in tears. My friends always help me through all of my problems and I'm blessed to have supportive family and friends. I've gone through a lot the past few years, whether it be my dad getting deployed several times, friendships destroyed, moving every couple of years, or drama after drama after drama. This one time last year, I was even getting hit and sometimes touched on my way home from school by an older boy. Most of it is just stuff people have to go through. My friends always support me. The ones that are meant to be my friends are still in my life. The ones that aren't meant to be my friends aren't anymore. I'm starting to figure out who my real friends are versus not real. It's a long and difficult process, just like finding out who you are.

I live a real life. I'm not fake in any way, unless makeup counts. I go through all the experiences most people do. I act myself, I don't change who I am just for others. I'm not popular and it doesn't matter. When you're popular, you have all the fake friends. They want to be your friend just because you're "popular". Well, guess what? After high school, you will have all your fake friends. I have real friends that actually care about my feelings and my grades and so on. I'm clumsy, shy, scared of the world, happy, sensitive, and strong.

BAXTER, 13

What is the thing that you take the most pride in? If you had to show one trait about you that would represent you as a person in this blobby mass of existence, what would it be? Your athleticism? Your charisma? Do you take pride in your pride? For me, it's my intelligence. My mind, my brain. It's what allows me to run and function as a human being. Not just function, but my basic personality. I have cultivated my personality as the person that knows everything. I am not infallible. I forget things. I don't know things. There are positive and negative results that spring from this. For one thing, when someone insults my intelligence directly, I can take it, and just disregard it entirely. However, if my intelligence is insulted indirectly, say I am very wrong and they mock me, I can't disregard it, for there is evidence in front of me. My mind is what I am. Technically speaking, a mind is what everybody is. A mind is what allows us as humans to experience anything. My mind has helped me. I keep good/decent grades and I feel that I am moderately intelligent. Often, when I was younger, I would correct my teachers. I still do occasionally correct my teachers. This tendency to be either an irritatingly sarcastic person or an absolute buzz kill springs from correcting people. The sarcasm comes from my cynicism, and my "buzzkillness" sprouts from my need to always be correct. This intelligence also allows me to be both incredibly self-aware, yet somehow incredibly forgetful. I know who I am, and all my mistakes, but my mind always seems to distract itself with whatever it can to distract from my flaws. And personally, I love it. It makes me, me, and more unique as a person. This also means I have a large ego. I am very aware, but my brain distracts itself from real problems, so I get false sense of self-importance. Some may call me vain because of this.

My family judges me silently. My mother is very argumentative so I try to argue sometimes. But she's still my mother, so even if I win, I lose. My dad is laid back but will sometimes be angry at me for being an indignant sarcastic (bleep). My brother is a very angry person so flaunting intelligence doesn't go so well with him. My younger sister is very annoying, and when I try to be intelligent she stares at me oddly. I often hide my sarcasm (mostly) around some of my older relatives. I will sometimes make a remark that some may say, "That's insulting," or, "Baxter!" or, "Stop, Baxter, it's her birthday, that's not very nice." Around my friends, my intelligence and sarcasm come full circle, with additional emphasis on sarcasm. Recently, I have found a new way to torture people with my intelligence: Puns. My brain finds word play and says it in a pun. Not only are they fun to do, but many people hate them. I kill two figurative birds with one stone by letting out cynicism and distracting my brain from my insecurities. It isn't the best system. It works, don't knock it till you try it, but it works. It's a makeshift way of doing things but-Oh look, a butterfly.

ADRIA, 14

I never tell anyone how I feel or what's bugging me because I don't want people to know. I don't need my parents knowing how I feel when they get in fights with their new partners and yell about how bad the other one is. Also, I have to keep my reputation as being a tough person and not caring about anyone or anything, because that's how I want to be. But it's not how I am. Pull down my wall and you'll see I'm a nature lover weirdo who wants people to like her, enjoys some things about school, is super emotional, wants to speak her mind but doesn't have the courage to, is super sarcastic, hates when people are upset, doesn't believe in herself, and gets lost in daydreams and stories.

I know I'm only fourteen and I don't have much life experience to go off of, but this is who I am today and how I envision I will be for the next year or so. Until I learn to grow positively and love myself-as everyone must learn to do-I can only hope I will encourage others to love themselves and throw away the mask.

CHAPTER 3

LIFE IN POVERTY

DANIELLE, 14

Living in poverty has allowed me to accept having little and wanting nothing. Having no money makes me more indecisive about spending money. When I go to the store, I end up not buying anything because I feel like I'm wasting money. Another thing that shaped me was growing up with my cousins when I couldn't make friends. It has allowed me to not care if I have friends because I always have cousins and other family members who love me. However, I also have a grandmother and grandfather that are married, but don't like each other, which has caused family members from each side of the family to not like each other. While I get used to it, it really makes me want to leave because I'd rather be alone. I am my true self with my cousins because it doesn't matter if I am crazy, calm, or quiet because I know I can be myself. Unfortunately, I can't be true to myself at school because I feel like they would make fun of me and not want to be my friend. I'd just rather keep a low profile at school and go be myself at home.

GREGORY, 14

I was born into a world of poverty. My mom was working for minimum wage while my dad was a nurse. My parents managed to keep me and my brother happy most of the time, but we lived in an apartment with only three rooms, along with having my grandpa live with us. My dad was gone a lot and my mom worked all day so my brother and grandpa were the only two people I could look up to. 50% isn't bad I guess. My brother is responsible for how I live, how I dress, how I talk, what I laugh at and what I don't laugh at. My grandpa is a different story. When he wasn't drunk he was kind, serious, and nice. But when you looked at him you saw a man whose life was troubled. He could be funny, but when he took to the bottle he was ignorant, impulsive, hard headed, and plain stupid. He verbally, and sometimes physically, abused my brother especially. I can remember bruises and blood on the floor. When grandpa would catch me disobeying he would spank me with his slipper or his belt. He would say two things in Filipino. One is, "you're in trouble," followed by a sentence that translates to, "I'm going to hit you." Memories of my brother's screams and whimpers still haunt me today. This all happened up until I was four years old. I think I gained some wisdom from my experiences. I have learned to be more careful of what I do and what decisions I make. It's led me to what I love the most and what I despise the most: family. A little passenger in the dark past has made me what I am, and allowed me to trust other kids who have dark passengers of their own. Whether it be divorce, drug addictions, or alcohol abuse, my friends all have an element of this darkness. But what makes them such great friends is that they harness their experiences into finding the light. We enjoy the good times, and we look out for each other.

ADAM, 14

I am unique in that I am Asian/German and was born 9 pounds 15 ounces. Yep, I was a big baby. Growing up was hard for me. We moved a lot because we always lived in homes we couldn't afford. My dad insisted on living in big homes, but we didn't have much money. Both parents worked low-end jobs, which made life pretty hard on me. I can remember them fighting about their lives and how they are failures. It was too hard for me to take so I had many teary nights. Since my parents didn't have much money, my sister and I didn't get much in the way of clothes or shoes. I can remember wearing the same pants and socks every day. I would get picked on and left out at school. Not having friends was hard on me. I would come home crying to my mom all mopey and angry because I was tired of getting left out. My mom hugged me tighter and tighter and told me to calm down. She took me to the kitchen for some chocolate milk to calm my nerves. She said to me the most inspirational, confident-building words anybody has ever said to me: "Adam. I know we are on a tight budget, and can't provide you and your sister with much food or clothes but that mistake is on me. I only have a high school degree and didn't go to college. I've regretted this my whole life. But I want you and your sister to be better than what your dad and I are. Get a college degree, and your life will open up. Try to be a leader, not a follower. Always try to be number one. I guarantee you, you'll live a better life."

Great advice, but there are some negative effects of my desire to be number one. I am a pretty good soccer player now and I hate it when we lose. We have to be number one, but when we're not I feel like I'm not the best. I become angry and can be a sorry loser because that's who I am. I'm trying to be better with that, but I've never been able to shake it.

CHAPTER 4

ALONE

ANDY, 13

Do you know how it feels to be alone at home as an 11-year-old with a younger brother and sister after your mom leaves for days before coming back? It's scary and horrifying. You feel like you want to throw up and you're scared she may never come back. You strive to do something better with your life, and you never want to be like that person because that feeling is traumatic to a child. There was no silver lining in this case. She did come back, but it was such a bad scene we had to live with my grandparents, which was even worse. We were stuck living in a house full of drunks and abuse. You're not supposed to live in a home where you don't feel safe, or where you cry every night because all you want is your mom to hold you and tell you she loves you with all her heart. I did not have that. In the end all you have are feelings of loneliness and abandonment, and all you are left with is yourself and your mind.

**INA, 14

My so-called rebellious phase, which people could interpret as "being lost" started in the summer of 2011. My then-17 year old brother had gotten his girlfriend pregnant the end of their junior year of high school. My brother, Jonah, had gotten a scholarship to Chaminade University in Hawaii. To any student on Guam, getting accepted to Chaminade let alone getting a scholarship was one of the highest brag-worthy achievements a Guamanian kid could receive.

Most Guamanian families are on the lower to middle class side of the economy, with children receiving barely subpar education and only the wealthiest of families who have connections to the government of the Island got into the private schools, where everyone has an Ivy League aspiration. But the truth is, the majority of the most promising students end up stuck on this dinky island, going to community college, or sadly drop out with 3 kids by the time they're 23. Jonah was one of the lucky ones. He was a scholar athlete, made varsity football, rugby and baseball since he was a freshman. He was also liked by everyone and surrounded by a loving and supportive family. He was the Golden Child of the family, and I, then 7 years old, sister to the superstar athlete, lurked in his shadows.

I was always acknowledged as "Jonah's little sister". I was hardly ever called by my actual name besides my family. Because of the fact that my parents were more interested in their first born child's life, I was on my own a lot. As a result of being alone, I would go over to my neighbor's house constantly. We had all grown up together so we were tight, but because there wasn't much supervision, I was exposed to marijuana at the tender age of 8. While all of my peers were playing house or with their stuffed animals, I was in my 15-year-old neighbor's room, taking a hit off a bong for the first time. Two, maybe three times a week while my parents were at Jonah's football games, I would ask to hang out with Raina, my neighbor who was around the same age as me, when I was really going into her older brother's room smoking weed or taking ecstasy pills.

When I was high, I didn't think I was in the shadows of my perfect brother. I was my own person. All the internal pain faded and I was content, filled with peace and relaxation.

Life went on. I went to school just because I was forced to. I wasn't the outgoing, social person I am now. I did my school work, got straight A's because my brother always had a 4.0 so the same was expected of me. When I came home from school, the house would always be full of my brother's friends who don't even know that I exist, do my homework, then go to Raina's house and take two pills of Molly, get high, then go back to my house for dinner where the only conversation is my parents talking to Jonah about school or his friends or what new award he received this time. I was the forgotten one, left alone to pick at the food I was given, without even a "How was school Ina?" Jonah's life was bright and exciting while mine consisted of drugs and dread.

Fast forward to my brother's junior year in high school. I walked into the door of my home to my brother sitting across the dining table from my mom and dad. Jonah's head is in his hands, my dad bursting out of his chair, the legs scraping along the floor, peering over Jonah and screaming a bunch of incoherent swear words. It was a muffle, with the only clear phrase I heard was, "Dacia's pregnant."

You heard it, the Golden Child got his high school girlfriend pregnant at 17.

Since Jonah had gone to an all-boys catholic school, his girlfriend Dacia went to a different school in a different village and since they had not been dating for long, my family had not known her or worse, the eventual damage her and her deranged mother would cause the Maktus family's immaculate reputation.

Some stories you've probably read say that the son is disowned or kicked out of the house because of a situation like this, but my parents knew what the probable effect of kicking Jonah out would do to their name. The whole island would soon be focused on the lead story: "Maktus Family Scandal: Golden Child Isn't So Golden Anymore". Fortunately for Jonah, my parents were smarter than that. He continued to go to the same expensive private school and drive a big flashy car. Nothing had changed. There was no conflict following the announcement of the pregnancy.

Around that time I had a moment to myself in the back of my yard, playing with my pet bulldog, Sandy, a light bulb finally lit above my head and my sanity had returned.

"What the heck is wrong with you child?" I thought to myself. "Hanging around that tug of a neighbor, doing stuff, some people don't do until they are in college? The family basically has one huge issue hanging above our heads, they don't need an 8-year-old drug addict added in the mix." It may be hard to believe but I had no problem stopping. After that "life changing" moment, I just stopped going over to the room that served as both my peace and kryptonite.

Anyways, when my brother's son, Samuel, was born, life somehow changed for everyone including me. My parents miraculously started paying more attention to me. They stopped comparing me to Jonah, but they still held the same expectations because as siblings, my brother and I were relatively close intellectually. It's fortunate I have always liked learning. Jonah and I even spent more time together, playing the same sports, going to the beach together, and taking me places he usually went with his friends. Dacia and I also got along really well since she was the closest thing I had to a sister. It especially helped that we all shared the same unconditional love for Samuel. Life was fine and dandy until one night, Jonah and my mom got into a heated argument about some irrelevant reason I can't recall, but it was bad enough that as a result, my brother took Dacia and Samuel and snuck them out the back door and ran away to Dacia's house in the middle of the night. I witnessed it all… and I didn't try to do anything to stop them. I just let my mom wake up to a house with her son and grandson missing and I kept my mouth shut and let her find out on her own that they went to Dacia's house on her own. Both my mom and brother needed to cool down and think about the irrational decision they both made. Over the course of the four-day separation, I asked to visit the house so I could spend some time with Samuel. During those 24 hours, I didn't eat a single item of food, not even a crumb. My brother didn't eat anything throughout the four days! Dacia's family was a low income family because her mom was a single parent to about 7 kids, 3 of which are not even hers. Which is why my brother came to the conclusion that it wasn't healthy for his family of three to be living in those conditions.

After a thoughtful make up between Jonah and mom, the three of them came back to live with us, and once again, life was back to normal, or as normal as a family in our situation could consider.

Then my dad was offered a life changing offer to work in the United States (state of Washington). After about a month after the job announcement, we came to a family consensus that it would benefit my brother, Samuel, Dacia and I to move for the reasons that the education system is 110 times better than Guam will ever be, and since Samuel and I have a skin condition called eczema, the cooler weather would help our skin in wondrous ways. Of course the money was much better too.

Of course life can't go this smoothly, right? On the night of January 17th, 2012, Dacia and Jonah walked into the dining room to have yet another maddening announcement.

"My mom doesn't want me or the baby to go to Washington with you… so we're staying here and Jonah is going with you guys." she said with her head down staring at the table the entire time.

It's hard to describe just how mad and heartbroken my brother looked at that moment in time. Dacia's mother had always been envious of our family. We had money, land, connections and because of my mom and dad's hard work, we had the support and attention of basically the entire Island. Everyone knew and respected us, but we did not take that for granted. My mom always said, "Your name is all you have." That's one reason why I am the person I am today, because I have lived off of that saying and to this day, I act the way I act so I can gain the trust of people. Six months into the school year, I had finally adjusted to typical American normality. But the thing is, is that I had only made a handful of friends, but I could never trust anyone fully, so I was alone again. My brother had it rough, living several thousand miles away from his son and the love of his life, and that stress and sadness affected me because I was so close to my brother and my heart hurt seeing him in pain. But one day he had had enough, he told our parents that he was going back to Guam to be with his family, and we understood that, so he moved back in a matter of two weeks, he found a job but was still struggling to support his family. During that time I had never felt more alone. I became a loner, awkward and depressed. And if it wasn't for one of my brother's friends, I wouldn't be sitting here typing these words. He walked into my room while I was tying a rope around my neck to hang myself in the closet. He saved my life and after, we had about a 3 hour conversation where I told him EVERYTHING. He was the only person at the time who I trusted completely. Still to this day he has kept his promise to not tell any living soul about what he walked in on. He was the person that helped me realize what a great life I could have. My parents are the most supportive and attentive they have ever been. I now embrace my bubbly, outgoing, weird and loving personality because I realize I am the way I am because I pushed through those unfortunate times and relied on my amazing friends and family to have my back and bring me out of my dark times.

****SO A, 14**

I honestly know how I made it this far with everything that has happened in my life. I am the way I am because of pain. I don't understand why I am bullied or why people have died or abandoned me. Losing the ones you love the most along with your mom being sick her whole life can change a person and her perspective. I've lost 15 family members in two years and my dad isn't around because of the military. Being bullied is the cherry on top.

In 6th grade, when I moved to California my dad got in a car accident, my mom had cancer, and everyone hated me. When I say they hated me, I mean every day the students would harass me and make me sit alone in a bathroom stall to eat my lunch. I was pulled out of my chair and the teacher accused me constantly of being a cheater just because she thought I couldn't be trusted. She constantly liked playing with my emotions. When I went to the counselor I'd had it with the constant name callings such as, "dirty white slut". Six students accused me of stupid things and the counselor believed them and told me I was in the wrong and I was falsely accusing them of bullying. Now I'm too scared of reporting to anyone. To this day I'm still bullied.

When everything got bad, cutting myself with safety pins was the only way I was able to handle my pain. I just built up a wall and masked everything. I've had a permanent fake smile ever since.

Last year, coming from all this pain and heartbreak, I got into the wrong crowd and got involved with the wrong people. There are these people who harass me daily who are supposed to be my friends, but take all their anger out on me. The girl who is kind, sensitive, and is on all the teachers' good side has a dark secret: I'm not fine.

I have always wanted people to like me. I want to fit in but the only ones who relate to me are older guys and adults. It doesn't help that I don't have much structure at home. My step-family doesn't like me much and the only family members that loved me the most died. I started starving myself because I was told how fat I was with the kids my age.

It is pure madness when your only friends you have to talk to are the monsters in your head. If you are alone with just yourself for too long you get to the point where you end up in an alternate reality where you name the people and you play with them inside your mind because the world around you seems to be burning. Although they would make me starve, lack sleep and cause me to fake everything and build up a wall, they seemed to be the only people besides my mom that would listen to me. Although my mom has fought most of my battles, the guns and battlefields in my head is the one thing that even I strive each day to extract. I lived in this daze of pure isolation and I could only dream of acceptance and worth.

I truly do believe that something good will come out of this, but I don't know what to hope and look forward to. One day I do believe that it will be easier for me so now I'm just waiting for that moment to come where I won't be afraid of being in the dark anymore.

SIMONE, 13

Life is complicated. I realized this as I write the fourth draft of this paper. Life is compiled of many things, including being influenced by others. I never thought my habits were from things I lived with, but as I flashback my whole life, I realize it's true. You wouldn't think bullying starts at first grade, would you? I didn't even know what the word meant then. I was in a multi-age class and the older kids in the class loved to bully me. One girl created barriers between me and the rest of the kids. I was miserable and couldn't do anything about it. My parents' advice didn't work. Sucking it up was all I could do. I remember a certain time at recess when everybody was playing a game. Apparently you had to have a secret password to play. Everyone refused to give me the password. That day I truly found out what "alone" meant. I hated being the "alone" kid. How could I ever trust anyone again? Fortunately, good news came when my dad told me we were transferring to

Washington State. Most kids hate moving for obvious reasons, but I literally was being saved by the Evergreen State. I loved the little town I'm in, I loved my elementary school-I've exceeded in school and never really looked back. I guess you're never free and clear of issues, though. My battles started with typical family stuff: My parents started to get stricter when I was in the fifth grade. My older brother was in ninth grade and his poor grades were stressing them out and they, in turn, pushed that stress onto me. I also started to feel the pressure of standardized tests at school and the expectations put on me. My stress level skyrocketed as I got older because the tests became more challenging. I was so focused on my school that I didn't look outside my bubble. Outside that bubble included my grandparents. I never called them and I totally ignored their existence. When they both died, I was struck with overwhelming feelings, especially when I saw my mother break down. I shouldn't hide the true me. Nobody should. I now realize how influenced I am by the people around me and that other people are going through the same issues as me. I have a crazy life, but I'm just glad I ended up here.

STEPHEN, 13

I only trust myself when I am alone because when I am true to myself at school, I get made fun of and called names. It doesn't get any better at home. My mom has hit me, punched me, and choked me. She will tell me she never wanted me. I'm dumb, retarded, or stupid. My brother even rejects me, saying he doesn't want me at home. I've never had a dad that stays with me. The only true friend I have, Darnell, and his parents are my only sanctuary. But everything I've grown up with has put me down for a long time. I learned this year to stand up for myself more. I don't have to listen to my mom when she says I'm not going to be successful in life. I can turn the other way and be what I want. It doesn't matter what happens and how you were treated. At the end of the day, you are responsible for you and where you're going to be in your life.

CHAPTER 5

DEATH

LAWRENCE, 14

The passing of my dad has severely impacted my life. Before he died, he would always tell me about needing to take school seriously or I'm gonna end up a bum on the streets. So, as a kid you normally don't like to listen to what your parents say. I didn't listen and my grades went down. After he died, I started to think about all the stuff that he had told me. I started doing better in school and paid more attention to my teachers. Then Richard Sherman, of the Seattle Seahawks, came to my school and he inspired me to do better in school. He gave me a pep talk to pay attention to my teachers, and keep my grades up. I've also realized that I don't have to be someone else that I'm not in order to fit in. I realize my teachers and friends like me for who I am, and I like me too.

SARAH, 14

When I lost my grandmother, I lost the inseparable bond we had. Don't get me wrong, we had our disagreements, but no matter how severe it was, we always found a way through it. She was my best friend and someone to whom I could tell anything trusting. She was the sweetest, most down-to-earth person you'd ever meet. She took pride in everything she did, touching lives each every day through her job as a social worker for 20+ years. She woke up every day at 5 a.m. and came home around 6 pm. She proved she was a hard worker and very dedicated to what she did. She didn't like when people were worried about her, and she always was the first person to ask, "how you doing?"

During the first stages of her being sick, nobody knew she held off on going to a hospital because she didn't like them. When she was finally diagnosed with breast cancer, her body already was shutting down. Three days later she passed away. My family was devastated, lost, and hurt all at the same time. When we lost her, everything started going downhill. Four months prior to her death, my 7-month-old cousin died from SIDS. After losing his mom, my uncle started taking to the bottle and has shifted away from the family. My mom is getting married, which is a happy event, but she is sad because she won't have her support system by her side to guide her along the way. Now without a wife, my grandfather has been overcome with sadness and grief. This has changed who he used to be. Pain is tearing my family apart. I feel like I'm the same person I have always been, only now it is accompanied by more emotions and sensitivity. I'm scared that I will be let down from showing how I feel to the wrong person, because my own family has let me down. From this I realized I wanted to surround myself with people who have goals in life and are always looking for ways to better themselves while also helping others. I've yet to find somebody like me, but that's a good thing because I am a one-of-a-kind. I'm happy for the most part when I'm around my friends. It's refreshing to be surrounded by people who accept you for who you are.

LOUISE, 13

How does anyone deal with death? I've had a hard time dealing with it. I'm not good with goodbyes or the death of loved ones. I am always hyped up and happy looking, though people don't understand some of the pain I feel inside. I may act happy but it doesn't mean I am happy. Maybe that's why I want to be an actress when I grow up. I love the idea of taking on a different character/persona. My friend motivated me to try out for a play and I fell in love with it. It was a small role, but I made the best of it. When I act I feel like a whole different person. I am weird, quirky, funny, mean (sometimes), but some people don't understand me. Doesn't phase me though. I will always be me.

CHELSEA, 14

Insecurity, courage, and depression are what shaped me. It started back in 2008. My brother, two sisters and I were taken away by Child Protective Services (CPS) because my parents didn't take us to school. The state started charging my dad fine money under The Becca Bill, which ensures all children are entitled to an education. My dad didn't pay, and every time the school came to our house, my dad would not open the door for them, so CPS came to our house to take all of us away for good. When they came, it was like my whole world stopped, and everywhere I walked, my life was falling apart. It was possibly the worst day of my life. CPS had placed us in my great aunt's house. We all didn't really like her because she was way too strict, but we got over it. To this day we still don't like her, but if it wasn't for her taking us into her home, all of us would have been put into a foster home and split up. In 2009, my grandma died and my dad did not take it very well because he loved her so very much. He was breaking stuff, hitting the walls and all that. After her death, my dad's life turned for the worse, resorting to drugs because he couldn't take the pain knowing his mom had passed. That year my little brother Devon was born. When he was born it was like everything good had started happening and everything was falling back into place. My aunt let us go to my dad's for the weekend to visit, and we got to see my mom on Sundays from 12-5 at her mother's house. Though my mom got a new house on a lake, my aunt still didn't let us go to my mom's house because of her baby daddy, Brian. Brian was violent and disrespectful towards my mom. A year and a half later, after being evicted from her home, she moved back in with her mom. My older brother dropped out of school and then when he turned 18, moved out of my aunt's house, and moved back in with my dad. Soon , after my little sister Elizabeth was born and she was awesome and so cute. I adored her. She looked just like her dad, but she also looked just like me in a way. In 2014 my sister Alexis graduated, making her the first in our family to graduate high school. She also moved out and back into my dad's house. I was very upset because it felt like she left us behind, even though we saw her on the weekends at my dad's. More tragedy followed early in 2016 when my aunt and uncle were involved in a fatal car accident. When we found this news out we did not know who died and who was alive because no one would tell us. We found out my uncle had died at the scene and my aunt was in the ICU with a broken neck, broken legs, and broken ribs. I kind of felt like my whole world stopped again. I was thinking about how everyone says everything happens for a reason. But nothing like that should happen for a reason. And the guy who was driving was my uncle's buddy and he was amped up on heroin at the time. He even had the nerve to move my uncle's body into the driver's seat. I still see Nick in my dreams or out on the water, because we used to go swimming all the time with him. He meant everything to me, he was the best uncle ever. I miss him, I really do. I loved him. All these things contributed to poor grades and attendance. But, while I let these tragedies impact me, I realized I couldn't let them be excuses for not following my own dreams. I learned it's best to not let the little things affect your schooling. Go do something with your life. For me, that's becoming a nurse and hoping to help as many people as I can.

JACINTA, 13

Ever since I was a baby, my mom and dad have been divorced. It's still hard going back and forth between homes. I have had anxiety for a very long time, but I've been able to keep a handle on it. I am also an only child, which has made me that stereotypical shy person. Making friends is one of the hardest things I deal with in life. I used to have a friend, Tyler, since we were babies. His mom and my mom were both friends. He was the only person I felt comfortable talking to. He also moved a lot, but I still got to hang out with him and his siblings. In kindergarten, I managed to make some friends, but I didn't talk to them that often, I would usually wait for them to talk to me. At recess, I would really only walk around or talk to one of the recess teachers. I was also trying to fight off the anxiety, which was very hard for me. I finally made another friend in second grade and we became friends for a few years until she had to move to England. During that year, Tyler had moved again. I got to visit him and his family a few times and they came to visit me and my family too. Later on that year, during school my teacher delivered some bad news. She told our class that something bad had happened to Tyler. There was a story of him climbing a tree with his scarf on and he accidentally fell and hung himself. After school, I got picked up by my mom and I remember her telling me the same thing my teacher said. She told me she did get to visit Tyler in the hospital. While on our way home, she said that my dad was going to meet up with us at our apartment. When we got there, we went inside and both of my parents sat on the couch and looked up at me. One of them said that Tyler was dead. I just looked at them with nothingness. I couldn't understand what they said. I could tell they were both very upset. Still, I just stood there trying to understand what they said. After my dad left to go home, my mom and I hung out for the rest of the night. When it was time for bed, I didn't go to sleep, I couldn't sleep. I told my mom about my trouble, so she decided to read me some books until I fell asleep. I never did go to sleep, and a few hours later I just burst into tears. I kept saying I can't sleep, I can't sleep, I can't sleep. Eventually, around three or four in the morning, I fell asleep. A couple days later at school, the counselor came to the classroom and invited everyone that was friends with Tyler to talk about the day. All of us went into one of the offices at the school and talked about all of our memories with Tyler. It was kind of sad, but also fun at the same time. I got to talk and I felt more outgoing. For a while at school all I could hear people talk about was Tyler, and saying false statements about how he died. It was really getting to annoy me. I was glad when it was all over with and I could forget the whole situation. After a couple of months my mom and I agreed to move into a new house with Tyler's mom and his two other siblings. His mom was going through a rough time, so we wanted her to feel better. I had such a good time living there-it felt like I had people to hang out with, and it was a nice house. We lived there for a while, but my mom was getting concerned about our roommate. She was very depressed about losing her son, and started doing drugs because of her loss. My mom got stressed and started to worry. She didn't want me near any of that stuff. So finally she found a nice apartment for us to live in. I was sad that we had to leave, but it was for the best. Thankfully Tyler's mom recovered. Losing one of my closest friends was a big change and a big loss. Since then I have had bad anxiety, but I have learned to get over it. I have also made a lot more friends and I can communicate with people better. My best friend still lives in England, but she is coming back home soon, which I'm very excited for. I have also made some more friends that have helped me with my anxiety. They have helped turn me into a very outgoing person.

SAFFRON, 14

If I know one thing, it is that death can be very hard. I grew up surrounded by it, wrapped around me like a blanket I couldn't discard. When I was a kid it's all I thought about. But when you have no idea how your own father died, it's excruciating.

All I really know is that he had his first child in September of 1988 and his last, me, in December 2001. My father had a passion for traveling the world and his favorite place was Phoenix, Arizona. He lived there for nine years before moving back to his hometown in Washington, where he met my mother in 1998, when he was 35. Then on May 31, 2001, he died. Life went on and my mother took care of three children: me (14) my brother (13), and my sister (3). 14 years of life and I am still left wondering who my dad was and how he died. When I ask about him I'm given the *"you're too young to understand"* speech and a look that's so pitying it hurts. Her refusal to give me any information about him is the biggest reason I don't have a good relationship with my mother. I currently have a step-dad, but ever since he came into my life we have butted heads, and our personalities and sense of humor is so different that we can rarely talk without getting angry at each other. Some days, it seems like we avoid each other just to keep our sanity. Growing without a positive relationship with my immediate family has put a damper on my youthful life.

Sometimes all I can think about is my father and how I will never get to meet him, never get to hear his laugh. I will never get to know why everyone says we look exactly the same. And I will *never* get to call him "dad" to his face. This has been a hard thing to come to terms with in my life and has taken me a long time to really accept. I will never know my father and that will never change, but it has affected me because people that I have known for a while have judged me for my feelings about something so uncontrollable. It really is true how people take things for granted. Once, I experienced these two kids trying to one-up each other on whose father has it worse.

"My dad is divorced."

"Well, mine is in the military."

"Mine works in a dead-end job."

Now, yes, I know that these facts probably make their relationships harder than it should be, but all I could think about was how they actually had a dad with them, and how I would give anything to have this man back in my life. They are so blind to see how lucky they are to have what they have.

Throughout my life, I have done countless research on my father, trying to understand who he was and how he died. I looked and looked, but nothing ever came up. Every day I would come home and look up his name, or his family and I could only find the surface information like his birthday and addresses. I researched for four years until one day a thought rattled me to my core. I always thought maybe he died of something shameful, like drugs, and that was why my family would never tell me, but what if it was hereditary? What if the thing that he died from could afflict me? I stopped looking after that day.

So, life went on and I began ignoring all the thoughts I had before about him, and almost altogether blocked him out of my memory. His death had me so confused and worried that I never wanted to think about him again, until about a year ago. I was talking with my sister about the death of my father, and she admitted to me that she believed he died of AIDS. This horrified me and I immediately denied it because of the things that I knew about the disease, so I blocked that out of my memory like the rest of my father and all the information I had built up over the years. For months, this idea was clouding my brain and I started second-guessing my health. It had me so stressed out that it was hard to focus. I later learned that it doesn't always pass through hereditarily. Although I have yet to tell my parents about me and my sister's hypothesis about my father's death, I believe with all my heart that his death was caused by AIDS.

Every day I learn more about him through myself. My mother has given me several pictures of him and has also told me more about him and what he was like. My dad may not be with me physically, but I believe he is with me in many other ways. He is part of me-it shows in the way I smile, the way I laugh, and in my eyes and my compassion. I wouldn't have it any other way.

CHAPTER 6

FAITH

ZANDER, 13

Allergies suck! Because of all my allergies, I have to be more cautious of what I eat and drink. But even worse, I even have to pay more attention to who's around me and who I hang out with because of a deathly allergy to peanuts. My alertness to this has also made me more observant of my friends and choices they make. I have also been impacted by becoming a Christian. The first thing I had to do was purge all my un-Christian music. I've also had to change the way I live and what I do. Before, we were what I would call a normal family with no beliefs. Now we go to church every Sunday and Wednesday. Now I live by stricter rules on top of the rules I already had to follow. We even went to church on Super Bowl Sunday. I have been grounded a lot more because of these serious changes. It's harder living as a Christian than being an atheist. This has caused an identity crisis for me. Where I live now is a lot better than where I lived in my previous town. I can trust my friends here, but my identity with them is different than who I really am. I act like an extrovert with certain friends, but I am an introvert around other people. At least I feel less pressure at school (I have less weight on my shoulders) than at home. At home, I'm simply a fake.

LASSANDRA, 13

I never thought getting baptized at the age of 12 would help shape me into who I am today. Knowing that I was going to get dipped in water was nerve-wracking. While I was getting prepared, thoughts were swarming through my mind. How long was I going to be in the water? Do I need to say a speech before being dipped? Am I going to enter and exit the right way? These were just crazy and unreasonable thoughts. All that worrying and thinking went away when I got dipped. I felt like a completely new person. Being lifted out of the water took my anxiety away. I was left feeling new and refreshed, figuratively and literally. Judgment is a very dangerous game. It used to be something I feared. But I couldn't be fake. I'm happy with my identity. I know I get judged and can be taken advantage of, but I've learned that's part of life because we're all human. My friends affect me on a daily basis, but only in a positive way. It can be frustrating seeing friends hold back. When I try to be nice to people, they push me away, but I don't take it personally. I think they're just too afraid of letting people in. Everyone has a story. We shouldn't have to judge them based on their differences. But that's just reality.

PAISLEY, 14

I would describe me as a go-big-or-go-home, happy, energetic child. I'm happy, energetic and loving life more than ever. I attribute this to my friendships and my newfound faith. August 15, 2015 will always be the day I was born into a new life. When I came home from a Christian retreat I realized what I experienced was a wonderful glimpse into Christianity-despite enduring a stinky, hot, eight hour bus ride to a desert with like-minded kids. My life is best described as the opposite of depression. I can't help but think positively, I can't help but see the good. I was never able to feel this kind of life before (even though I've always been happy). I look the same on the outside, except for, you know, puberty. But my soul changed. I have a lot to learn and a lot to see and I can't wait. My life will never be the same. I have friends like I've never had before, but most importantly, I developed a relationship with my permanent best friend, God, and I met a new me in the process.

SHARRY, 14

I'm asked to sit here and type up what makes me, well, me. That's a pretty loaded question. I guess I will just start by saying a few facts about me. I am the oldest in my family so I enjoy being the first to do pretty much everything, but there is also a lot of pressure on me to do everything right. I know my parents don't mean to, but they put so much pressure on me to be the best and have the best grades. Sometimes it's hard to keep up. But don't get me wrong, I love my parents and they are very supportive, but they were expected to do a lot at a young age so they do the same to me. My family life isn't what made me the way I am though.

This year, a lot happened. Most of it is still going on though. To sum it up, I had this best friend and then I started getting feelings for him. Then he started dating my other best friend. Now this is neither of their fault, and I never told anyone the way I felt because I did not want it to be weird. A little while later, my best friend and I get really close, so I tell him I like him, and then he tells me to tell his girlfriend so that there are no secrets between us. I tell her and she says, "It is fine. You cannot control who you like." Everything was fine for a while, until each of us felt jealous about the other. Then we just blew up. We all said stuff we didn't mean. A little while later I apologized, although I didn't really feel like I did anything wrong. We became friends again, then stopped being friends, then I apologized and the cycle kept repeating itself for a while. New Year's Eve came along and my church said that I needed to remove everything toxic from my life. I texted my friend and told her that I will miss her, and I wished her the best but we couldn't be friends. She agreed and that was it… at least, that's what I thought. After that, all of my friends blamed me for ruining our friend group. At this time I felt really alone. I never wanted to go to school because I didn't even know if I had any friends. Then one day my youth leader reached out to me. It brought me to an amazing group of friends, who made me feel more positive and confident. I wanted to learn and explore, and best of all I developed a better relationship with God. I learned it is okay to break down, but it's not okay to stay down. I realized God is bigger than any problem I could have. Now I can easily say that I am happy, and I have found friends who are always there for me, care about me, and want to see me succeed. My bit of advice I can pass on to others is that your so-called enemies hate to see you happy, so pick up your head, smile, and even though it might be hard, be nice to them. You only have 100 years max on this earth. Why spend that time pulling someone else down?

CHAPTER 7

A SHAPED ENVIRONMENT

**VIOLET, 14

I'm not real, especially around most of my family and the people at my school. That's okay because I have people and the internet I can be real around. I feel enclosed at home. I haven't had much room to grow and since I was real little I've internalized a lot and handled my problems on my own. It's how I thought the world worked and that's why I'm so *"secretive"* and can't talk to my parents about the small things. My friends have always been real with me, so I try to be as authentic as possible. To be fair, I don't know me very well either.

I'm still exploring myself and the world. At least I have plenty of time to figure out exactly who I am. Right now I'm a 14 year-old who aspires to be a singer, writer, barker assistant, day care assistant, and YouTuber. Maybe that's a bit too much, but I can fantasize, right? My main goal is to probably be a YouTuber, though.

I'm fake with everyone, including myself. I try to act like more than I am and take on more than I can because I'm *"strong"* and *"tough"* that way. It's actually stressful. I try my best most of the time because I don't want to disappoint anyone, though I feel I do most of the time. I tell myself lies about myself and I disappear to other realities because I hate this one. I try to escape, but all I'm doing is lying to myself and making myself feel worse. It's my only escape, so I do it.

I was never really one for social interaction, sadness, or other people's problems as a kid. Mainly because I didn't understand it and didn't want to have to deal with it. I just wanted to run around carefree and do what I wanted. Granted, my parents never really let me do that. They wanted to keep me safe and to let me explore, but they never really gave me the chance. Because of them, I am a more cautious person. I get injured quite a lot, but my injuries aren't what falls under my caution. It's hard for me to swim, skateboard, build things, explore, and wander because my parents never gave me the opportunity to try those things. I was simply taught manners like how to clean, how to cook, and how to function as a person in society. They gave me different aspects of different things, like the chance to follow in music, art, dance, theater and writing. They taught me how to ride a bike and so on. They just never gave me opportunities to find the different daredevil parts of me. Plus, as I was growing up they warned me about the people around us. Because of that, I'm suspicious and untrusting, which I feel I should not be, but I am.

**CARTER, 14

As a child, I was pushed to have the greatest grades possible, well at least in elementary to have all "4"s. Even now I am pushed to have all A's. This is all because of my mom, who is overprotective, but wants what's best for me. This is why I've been labeled as the "smart" kid. But I am active outside of books too. I love playing sports, going to the local water park and other adventures. Despite all that, kids at school don't really know the true "me". Even some of my friends don't know me.

They think I live a normal life. Yeah, they know I have loving parents and a younger sister. There are many not normal parts about me. But since 7th grade, I have been fighting a hidden battle with scoliosis.

Scoliosis is when your spine is curved to one side. I found out about having scoliosis when my mom noticed I had a hump on the right side of my back. (I guess I'm kind of like a hunchback) So, of course, being the mom that she is, she took me to the doctor to get it checked out. Turns out I had a 42 degree curve of my spine. I received a back brace around the end of Christmas break and it completely changed my life both at school and at home. At school, I was not as talkative and outgoing because I was self-conscious whether people could see the straps peeking out of my shirt. I thought that if I brought more attention to myself people may notice, so I stayed quiet. My silence made it to where I did not have as many friends, however, this only affected my school life, as I continued playing basketball and indoor soccer.

The silence remained all year and, like everyone else, was excited for the end of the school year. X-rays taken towards the end of the school year showed the curve didn't get any worse, so school started up again for 8th grade and, again, I remained the quiet kid in class hiding a back brace. The news during 8th grade wasn't good. The doctor said that my curve increased to 52 degrees. Surgery was recommended, which was heartbreaking since this meant no sports for six months.

Living with hardships is very difficult. Living with scoliosis is difficult, but it gets better because there is always a solution. For example, surgery is a good thing because it will fix my back and everything. In fact a few days ago I got some good news when the doctor said that the lower part of my back is almost all the way straight, which means I will have more flexibility in the long term. Just remember whatever your problem or hardship, it will get better.

LUCAS, 15

The first seven years of my life were a struggle. I was always getting kicked out of preschools, while my mom--being single 'n all--had to work to pay the rent and feed us both. We lived in a couple of different two-room apartments and I had very little idea of who my dad was. I don't really remember seeing my dad that much when I was that little but whatevs. When I moved up in the world of kindergarten, I have been always in the principal's office and later got expelled from the school. I was put into a behavior school in 1st grade and was diagnosed with "optimal defiance". The school was pretty fucked up. It was filled with kids with severe problems. They had a room with a Velcro latch to detain kids. I recall this one kid throwing a big rock through the window of the main office; glass shattered. Another time I was in the little room talking and I really had to use the bathroom. The adults in charge ended up not letting me go so after school I told my mom and she went off on the people in charge of that classroom. From there on out my mom and I have had a close relationship. But my life wasn't all sunshine and rainbows. Shit went downhill later that year when my mom married a manipulative military jackass.

We ended up moving in with him at Bangor Naval Base north of Silverdale. Oh yeah, I left out the part that we also lived with my sociopathic grandpa who was absolutely bat shit crazy and spoiled me like there was no tomorrow. At least I always had something to do or someone to hang out with while living on Bangor, but that soon ended, as my mom's husband (my "stepdad") got orders to move to Honolulu, Hawaii for three years. This turned out to be really good for me. I embraced a fresh new start. We also had new additions in the form of a little brother, and soon after, a little sister. My school life rapidly improved over the time I spent in Hawaii. Nothing really crucial happened in Hawaii until around the third year when my stepdad was hanging out with this crackpot friend. This other friend of his, Sean, started shedding light to us on how horrible a person my stepdad was. He was always really awesome to us and he had a lot in common with my mom. My mom soon filed for divorce and soon after that moved in with my grandpa back in Port Orchard. .It's during my time in elementary school, I met some of my closest friends that I'm still friends with. Sean married my mom and things seemed stable other than the fact I became insecure and self-conscious in middle school. I ended up getting into a small fight with someone and got suspended for about three days right at the end of first semester. My friends at school weren't the greatest; always doing dumb crap and drugs. It's a wonder I didn't get arrested in 7th grade. By the time eighth grade rolled around I was still hanging out with the same type of people and doing the same things. It wasn't till early in 8th grade October that things started to change. My best friend mentioned to my mom that I was going down a bad road and by the time I got in the car my mom knew everything. I wasn't really punished, but it definitely changed the way I saw things. I ended friendships with bad influences and reconnected with most friends from elementary school. I've been able to keep my grades up this year and I never got arrested (despite the shit that surrounded me) and I let myself get influenced (positively) by the music I listen to.

LEONARD, 14

I live in a very rural area with no neighbors, so I do everything individually or with my brother. Our parents want us to be responsible so they give us a lot of work around the house. They also have high academic expectations. We get punished for anything below a B. Another thing about our environment is I teach myself anything I want to know. This could be knife throwing, archery, rifle shooting, ATV riding, horseback riding, computers, robots, physics, and so on. Being raised in a smart family makes it easy for me to get frustrated at others who don't share the values that come with maturity and responsibility. I also credit Boy Scouts of America for shaping my life. I have learned countless skills over the years, having earned various merit badges. I'm also in a higher scouting organization called The Order of the Arrow. We perform Native American songs, dances, and ceremonies. Our main goal, though, is service projects for scouting and the community. As much as I value what I've gained growing up, my comfort level is strongest with my friends because they're simply more relatable than my parents. At home, I am quiet and conservative, but at school I can relax and have fun with my friends.

NICOLE, 14

I know it's cliché for a kid to say this, but moving sucks. I just moved up here from San Diego with my mom and dad because my dad works for the Navy base. The timing of the move was the worst part, since it was with one month left of school. I had to say goodbye to friends I'd had for the last five years. Tough to do that, especially since they helped me through so many things. Leaving them was the most painful thing I've ever had to do. It's hard for me to get California out of my head. I want to move back after high school. It's my home and it's all I know. Washington State is amazing, but it doesn't feel like home. It has helped meeting amazing people here. I'm just not a fan of change. My parents have been supportive of me and my new friends. The biggest challenge was catching up in school because the schools here are way ahead of the California schools.

AMALIE, 14

It might seem odd to some that I would complain about getting to live in other countries. My peers would say, "that's a gift," or, "why would you complain?" I shouldn't complain about getting to live in Japan and England, but being a "Navy brat" isn't all it's cracked up to be. If you aren't a perfect, well-disciplined child, you disappoint people and it reflects badly on your Navy parents. I've always been pressured to be good in any field they throw at me. What's funny is most of the pressure comes from my grandparents. They say to me, "be good at fishing," "don't play video games or they will rot your brain," or, "don't draw anime or cartoons because they aren't useful." It would be my job to tune out the constant chatter and continue what I love and want to do. Recently, disappointing people has been more of a problem. I've disappointed my grandma by not being "ladylike." Instead of women's clothing, I go for men's clothes and boy haircuts. I like to dress like a guy because it's simply more comfortable.

Being in the Navy is not an easy boat to ride. Despite disappointing people and making my family's life harder, I'm uprooted and forced to live in different places every five years. I have to start a new life and it only gets harder the older I get. I left friends over in England and miss them, but moving from there to here has changed my life and made me who I am. While it's not easy being uprooted, it has allowed me to see different worldly views and shaped me into a well-rounded person.

KELLI, 14

When I think of my "development" as a person, I don't think of a rough life like Ponyboy or any other underdog story. I think of years of family members' hospital visits, medications, and chemotherapy. My family has dealt with all medical issues since I can remember.

I was two years old when my Aunt Kari was diagnosed with Stage 3 breast cancer. I don't remember much of this time since I was so young. A year later, my Grandma Kathy was diagnosed with Stage 4 breast cancer. She showed me what it means to be strong. At this time, she was my neighbor and I would constantly be at her house, helping her in the garden, picking berries, or playing on the playground. She would always have a big smile on her face no matter what. We would make cookies and pies, and play board games in the living room with my two cousins, Campbell and Cole. When I was four years old, my Aunt Jeanne was also diagnosed.

As I grew older I still could not tell my grandma was slowly growing weaker and weaker. But it didn't matter how she was feeling, she always went to all my concerts, assemblies, and parties. She also would take me, Campbell and Cole to fun outings where we would drive to McDonalds to get milkshakes or go to the bowling alley. When I was six years old, my Aunt Mary was diagnosed, and I started to understand how strong my family members were. When I was seven years old, my Aunt Lisa was the last to be diagnosed.

At eight years old, I would visit my grandparents and Grandma would either be in a wheelchair or in her hospital bed in the living room. She would be connected to IVs, tubes, and other medical equipment, but she still had that shining smile on her face. I started to worry about her health. Then on a cold February day, which at the time seemed like any other day, my Mom had me sit down on the couch. I could tell she was upset and this scared me. She told me that Grandma had passed away peacefully and that everything would be ok.

My parents also have helped me down the path to a good successful life. They have told me from a young age that if I want to do something, I have to work hard and put in the effort to earn it. They have not only made me a hard working student, but have given me the skills to be whoever I want to be.

These amazing people taught me how to be brave, how to face my fears, and most importantly, how to be strong. When I am around my family I am 100% me! My favorite thing to do is hang out with them-it doesn't matter where we are as long as we're together. When I am with them, I can be totally and completely me.

When I am with my friends I am not as crazy as I am with my family, but I still make sure I am myself. On the soccer field, I am the best me I can be! I can rely on my teammates to have my back. My team is my family. Being with them is the highlight of my week. Some of my favorite memories are spending time with them on and off the field. Whatever challenges we face, we have and will always do it together. All of these people have gotten me to the person I am now, and these experiences will help me be the person I want to be.

DENISE, 14

Some people say I'm a scared kid. I don't know if it's true, so I don't know what to believe. My mom says I became a new person when I moved to Washington State. Mostly, I feel like I'm a big disappointment to my parents. If I do something wrong, I feel their disappointment. I'm already hard on myself, so imagine how I feel when they are upset with me. Moving has impacted me. Though I like new places, I hate leaving my friends. My dad being in the military sucks because I don't see him very much. While I am happy with who I am, I don't know who I am yet.

JOMAYRA, 13

I am a hilarious, Dominican, reader/writer and Puerto Rican who is stereotyped by people around me at my school, which forces me to wear a coat every day. It is not right to judge people. My home is in New York City-the amazing place with all my family and an all-girls charter school I attended, the mini-grocery stores with my favorite junk food, the awesome family I depended on and spent so much time with, my yearly visits to see my father, my white cat Bonnie, my comfy room, and my 3 best friends.

That all changed after a 7 ½ hour airplane flight from The Bronx to the state of Washington. Everything fell apart. This feeling of not being able to do anything, the thought of my friends and family forgetting about me, and my missing out on everything took a large toll on me. I began to stress eat, going to bed late, waking up super early, not doing my hair, and a pure hate for my sister and resentment towards my stepdad grew. The fake smile I put on for everyone sure fooled them. Now, I realize being too friend and family attached is a really bad habit, and that you should keep your family close and need them, but also take care of yourself. Now I remember that you need to be there for yourself no matter what, and guide yourself toward the direction of your goals.

TRASK, 14

I'm the guy who loves lacrosse. Ever since I was 10 years old, it has been my passion. I play goalie. My coach says I'm the best goalie in the state. I don't know how I got to this point, but I did, and am beyond happy with where I've come. My mom and dad got divorced when I was five. I have an older brother and sister. I grew up going to a Mormon church every Sunday. I still go, just not as much due to lacrosse and other complications. I'm the person who cares about everyone. My mom says I should do something later in life to help people. I like helping people, which is probably part of the reason why I like playing goalie. I always have the feeling I'm making a difference. I don't know where I would be if I would not have found lacrosse. A lot of people ask me why I love it so much, because to them it's just a sport. For me, it's more of a lifestyle-a lifestyle I can't live without. My brother, Arnie, is the one who taught me the sport I love. Arnie is going to Colorado this summer for college to play lacrosse. I can't explain all the many things he's taught me that I will forever be grateful for. My 16-year-old sister, Jaelyn, is the same way but with horses. She has won many awards with horse-related topics, but it doesn't end there. She is practically a professional photographer. She even has her own company. She takes pictures of just about everything, horses especially, and puts her photos into nationwide contests. She has won almost every time, if not every time. Just like Arnie, Jaelyn has taught me many life lessons. I have many friends, but I only have a few true friends that I know I can trust. I used to be fake with my friends, trying to fit in, but then I woke up. When I was younger, I would just do whatever everyone else was doing because I didn't know what life really was. I still don't know where I stand in life. I'm getting closer every day to figure out who I really am. I feel like I've been trapped inside a box all my life, protected by my parents and not trying anything new. I guess that can be good because my mom works in a hospital and has seen some of the horrible things that drugs can do to a person. I am happy with who I am. I feel like I'm heading on the right track, but I also have no clue where that track will take me.

GALEN, 14

Moving around a lot can have its disadvantages, but I tend to see it as a positive. I have gotten to see many different types of people, places, and things. With all the things I saw, I knew what kind of people I wanted to be around, and knowing who or what kind of people I wanted to be around helped me discover who I wanted to be. I always knew that I wanted to be athletic, and I also always knew that I didn't want to be a bully, and that I wanted to be kind and funny. I knew that I didn't want to be bullied because I did get bullied. One of the times that I remember specifically was the first time that I fought back. It was a kid with long hair who was shorter than me. He shoved me against a concrete wall and punched me in the stomach. Then I grabbed him by his long hair and smashed his face into the wall. From that day on I only lost one fight, but it was beyond my physical capabilities. I was at the playground with my cousin and this much older and bigger bully came up and shoved my cousin, so I shoved him back, and then he hit me and dragged me over to the soccer goal. He lifted me up and wrapped the net around my wrists so that I couldn't get down and then he punched me in the stomach and my cousin sat on the ground and watched. I don't let it phase me though. Nowadays I am athletic, have lots of friends, and I get good grades. How can a kid not be happy about that?

ABBOTT, 13

I have been moving all my life--a kid of the military. I have learned to become emotionally detached to the people around me. I don't share my secrets. I don't open up to people. This has helped me with the stress and heartbreak of all my moves, leaving everyone I cared about. From a young age, I have become "adaptable". I adapt to the people around me. For example, I am a totally different person to two different friends right now. That's why it's easy for me to make friends. My personality changes to match theirs. I guess they are not my real friends, seeing as they don't know the real me. But to be fair, I don't even know the real me. I have changed so much I don't think I have had time to grow as my own person. But I know my passions are a part of me. I love reading and Legos. When I read, I get sucked into a whole new reality--one where the characters become real. I feel what the characters feel and live what they live. I am still finding myself, but I know whoever I am, I will love it.

MIRABELLA, 14

This is for anyone out there affected by ADHD. On the outside I look the part of a quiet, shy and smart person, yet on the inside I have been living my entire life with ADHD. I found through research that if you were born prematurely and/or underweight, the chances of having ADHD go way up. I was born 6 weeks early at just 4 pounds 5.5 ounces. It seems like I was meant to have ADHD.

First grade was challenging for me because I could not focus and did not get work done. My teacher talked to my mom and told her about this. On top of not focusing, I could not sit still. I tried so hard, but it felt impossible because so many things were running through my brain. It felt like I was going 100 mph. I went to my doctor and almost right-three days later--the doctors diagnosed me with ADHD.

For five years my doctor tried lots of different kinds of medicines, but they all give me stomach aches, and the side effects did not help my ability to focus. I had a counselor in second grade that helped me deal and cope with my disorder, because I could not be in a crowded room or have someone sit one to two feet away from me. This led to bouts of anger, which again, I could not help. What a lot of people don't know is most people grow out of their ADHD by age 10 or 11. Not me. I still live with it every day. When anxiety kicks in I do breathing exercises that have worked since first grade.

Anxiety comes in different forms. For me it is stomach aches, feelings of being trapped, and becoming agitated easily. I am thankful to at least have the tools now to help me through my hard times. Another symptom of ADHD that I have is that my brain is three steps ahead of me. I will be working a step for a math problem, but my brain is already doing the next problem, which causes me to do my work incorrectly. Sometimes there is confusion between having ADHD or behavioral issues. The best way to describe the difference is that behavior is learned, but with ADHD you cannot control the way you act at times. You could have a meltdown, then be angry in a matter of seconds unless you have tools like I do, along with the right medication. When I was little I was ashamed of having ADHD. I never told anyone that I have it because I was afraid that they would treat me differently. It took me three years before I told my best friend, and she always keeps my secrets.

Over the many years only five of my friends are aware of it. Over time you could say I have become more comfortable in my own skin. I am confident and proud of who I am and why I am this way, no matter what people think or say. I will face many more obstacles in the years to come. If I did not face ADHD, I would not be who I am today. Some people may look at having the disorder as a weakness, flaw, or even a funny trait. They also may think that ADHD limits you and that you are not a very smart person. I also don't believe in making ADHD an excuse for struggling in school. I have A's in all my classes and I think having ADHD has helped me to reach this because I have to focus and try harder to do my work. Looking back to elementary school, I wish I was not ashamed of having ADHD, because I kind of hid in a shell and denied people the chance to know the real me. Now I have overcome my fear and am not ashamed of who I am. To my friends that know, I am Mirabella. I am not judged by my snort when I laugh, or my weirdness. They like me for who I am. As I said before, this is just the start of the lifelong journey of my life with ADHD.

CHAPTER 8

DIVORCE/ABSENTIA

**NATHAN, 15

We are told to appreciate everything our mother has given us. Appreciate her, treat her with respect, and love her. We even have a day to appreciate and celebrate mothers. People write full on paragraphs and essays and make gifts just for them. But do you know how uncomfortable and awkward it feels to be that one kid in class who doesn't know what to write about their mother? All I could do was write simply "Happy Mother's Day." People would ask me to write more, but I couldn't. I have never loved my mother. I never had anything good to say about her. She abused me; mentally, emotionally, and sometimes even physically. It started in the summer before I went into kindergarten. My cousins and my sisters had enough long hair and ability to cover their face while in a ponytail while they pretended to be the Grudge. My hair was too short to cover all of my face. I told my mother sitting on the couch in the living that i wanted to be like them, but she told me that I would never be like them. It's true now, but at that time the only thing I wanted was to be like everyone else and to fit in with the crowd. That's where it started and it only got worse from there. I remember being grabbed by the wrist tightly and thrown into the bedpost in my room while being called a "whore" and "slut" by the age of 8. Being set up for diets because my mom told me I was too fat at 9. Being told I was too dumb to go to college and I had to be a stay at home mom and possibly drop out because my grades were dropping and I had trouble to bring them up. I had become antisocial, insecure, anxious and even depressed at a young age. I bottled everything up because my mother told me that I'm over-dramatic about everything when I come home crying because I was being bullied. She cursed me out, told me that I will have to go back to church to fix myself when she found out I was attracted to girls and boys. Can you imagine this little kid standing in front of the mirror hating every single thing about themselves and thinking that they were broken, weird, and a freak? It's not something a little kid or anyone should think about when they look at themselves. When my dog, my best friend and only friend I had, died when I was in fifth grade, I had only realized then that I was being abused. I tried being like other kids all my life, but my mom yelled at me and sometimes even hit me when I didn't like her opinions, and whenever I wanted something that the "cool" kids had. My mom stopped letting me out of the house when she found out I snuck out to go to the neighbor's house to feel free and have fun for once. I couldn't even go to my grandma's house, the only adult I trusted at the time, to escape from my mother. When we had our house sold under our feet, we moved into her mom's house.

The abuse got even worse. I started failing classes more, she yelled at me, threatened me. I was the first to find out that my mom was cheating on my dad. It was about 4 A.M. and everyone was sleeping beside me because I had horrible nighttime panic attacks. I checked her phone to check the time and she had a message from one of her many boyfriends. I tried telling the whole household, but nobody believed me. I got cursed out by everyone. One day I tried stealing her phone to show them, but she got to me before I could show anyone. She slapped me really hard. I started tearing up a lot and I hid in the bathroom. That was my only chance to prove I wasn't a liar. I felt even worse. I got a couple of the hand held sharpeners from the desk and began trying to break and loosens the blades from it. I started cutting myself then. I felt like I deserved it. My parents never found out until July of 2015, just 4 months after we moved to Washington. That summer my mom threaten to kick me out of the house if I made one more mistake. It wasn't even her house; it was my grandparents' house. I hid myself more though, and I stopped talking to everyone.

Nobody cared that I started skipping meals or had gone days without food. They only got excited that I was losing weight. My dad was the first to find out I was cutting. I told him that mom wanted to kick me out, but he didn't believe me. He always told me that my mom loved me and would never do that. Well, she did, and it ruined me. If she really loved me, if she really cared, then she wouldn't have done any of what she did to me. When we moved to an apartment near my middle school, it got even worse again. Mom continued calling me names and they still really hurt. I moved up to seventh grade barely knowing anyone. I recognized just a few familiar faces from 6th grade, but I didn't really know anyone and they didn't know me. No one understood why I wore long sleeves in the hot weather. No one knew what was happening to me or what I was feeling. I got some help on social media from complete strangers. Complete strangers on the internet helped me to not try to kill myself or cut myself again. They listened to me when no one else would. But I never became real friends with them sadly. At the end of January of 2016, I did want to kill myself at the time and I was really tempted, but someone from school told the councilors and I got in massive trouble. I lied to my family and the school about why I wanted to do it. It wasn't because a kid called me fat. It was because my mom was abusing me and i wanted it to stop. I wanted the pain to stop, but no one would've believed me if I said she was the reason. According to my family she's always right and I was just the overdramatic liar.

Things got a bit better since then though. I had made a lot more friends. I finally found someone who believed me and not what my mom said for once and she has stuck by me for more than a year now. Throughout that year I still felt suicidal and cut myself now and then, but it did get a little better. When we moved again in October, it got bad again. I rarely stayed in the house. I stood outside in the freezing cold just so I didn't have to hear my parents fighting. I slipped into a bad spot, but my friends kind of helped me with it. My best friend and I were surrounded by bad influences and I realized that when it was too late. December through February were probably some of the hardest months for me. I cut myself a lot and my mom hurt me a lot more. She even tried to hurt my older brother and I'm pretty sure he still has a mark on his neck from it. I cussed out my mom, too. I hit her and called her the same things she's had been calling me for all these years, maybe even more. Everyone wanted her out. We tried kicking her out so many times, but she came back because my dad loved her. I hated that so much. I just wanted to yell at him that he's making a mistake, but I couldn't say a word and I kept biting my tongue. We finally kicked her out sometime in February. My friends and I were so happy she was gone. She tried to hurt one of my friends and my sister-in-law one night. I never wanted to hurt somebody so badly. Dead or alive, I just wanted her gone. I was so tired of her and her lies and everything that she has done. When we visited her for my birthday (I didn't want to go at all) we never lasted a day without fighting. I told them the truth that she was abusing me and she's the reason why I tried to kill myself and that she was a lying cheater. She denied all of it. She can't admit to anything she has done. How can she live with herself knowing she did all of that? I never answer her texts or calls and she blames it on my dad saying "he corrupted our little minds." But in reality our family knows what she did to me and what she did to my dad and I was the one who told everyone to stop talking to her. Nobody wanted her. Even her other boyfriends stopped talking to her. I was in control of what everyone else thought about her mostly. My dad gets upset that we don't talk to her, though, because he gets blamed for it even when I made it clear that it's my fault. I have to hear big arguments between my sisters about who will pick up the phone, because no one wants to do it.

So most of the time we pretend we're asleep and let it ring. We have completely disowned her from the family. I am a lot better now without her. Everyone is, but I still feel like she deserves a punishment; a punishment for abusing me. Kicking her out just isn't really enough for me. She's planning to take my younger sisters away, but neither of them want to leave. I tell my sisters every day that they are staying with me. I don't care what I have to do, but I will not let what happened to me happen to any other child. Most everyone believes me now, but my dad is still iffy about it. I'm trying to help make things right and I'm trying to follow my own dreams at the same time. I will not let her hold me back anymore. I'm finally getting good grades and I've gotten accepted into AVID. I'm on the pathway to following my dreams. I finally have something to look forward to. A future where I could be successful and maybe even happy finally. I have plans for the future that she cannot ruin anymore. People say I'm a lot like her, but that's really not true. I'm so much more caring, loving, kind-hearted, generous, accepting, loyal, and I know very well that I will be a better father and husband than she was a mother and wife. I am a lot better person than she is. I will never be her.

SHANNA, 13

My world is full of good and bad memories, but I can't shake the heartache my mother has caused me and my siblings. I try to remember the happy times, but it's hard to capture good times after my parents divorced when I was five years old. My mom just up and left with no explanation and no goodbye. What mother would do that to her children? Three years later she magically reappeared and told us she had taken care of things (issues). But only a year later she left again and I haven't seen her since (five years and counting). I'm glad because I don't want to see her again until she's fixed her life. But a blessing in my life has come in the shape of my stepmom. She has been there for me and helps me whenever I need it. She has a better perspective on life than my mom ever will. She makes sure I'm doing well in school, having fun, and staying out of trouble. She makes sure I have a roof over my head and a plate of food in front of me. She is simply amazing. My siblings are another story. I have a 12-year old brother who has a hard time breathing because of heart issues. My older brother (16) sometimes blames me and my sister for my mom leaving the family. We don't know where he gets that idea. I have a half-brother who is 18 but we don't see that much.

What I do know is that my mom's decision to abandon us is none of our faults. We shouldn't be hurt or sad about it, but it is always around us. We are able to try our hardest to move forward with our lives because we have an amazing stepmom who makes us laugh and smile every day. That's all that matters.

GRACE, 14

My life is definitely not perfect. I know that who I am today is not going to define me, but I know it is going to affect my life. The first defining moment in my life is when my brothers got taken away because my mom was arrested for a DUI. Even though my brothers aren't my full blood brothers, they were always my brothers. I have barely seen them the last two years. Mom's DUI also forced me to live with my dad, who was never really in my life. Living with him didn't work out well, so I moved to Port Orchard to live with my grandma.

My mom was with us briefly, but her life has spiraled out of control. Just two weeks ago, my mom was in the ICU near Tacoma because of health issues related to drug use. I almost lost her twice. Then last week my papa that she was staying with found her drugs. She got really mad about it and now she's left on the streets somewhere and I'm scared, because next time I see her, she will either be in jail, in an institution, or dead. On top of that, I deal with stupid teenagers on a daily basis. This school, like all schools, is filled with fake people and fake "homes" and fake words coming out of people's mouths. All I can do is wait for stability and pray to a God that I don't know yet and don't understand; hoping that maybe He will answer my questions, concerns and "prayers". Knowing that my mom--the only one who stayed with me through everything-- is out on the streets somewhere sucking the life out of herself with this pesky monster we call addiction is heart wrenching. She's already attached to two felonies and there's two warrants out for her arrest. You wouldn't know it because of her problems, but my mom raised me to be a strong person like she used to be. No matter who talks about my mom or puts her down in any way she will still be the best mom in my eyes. My anguish is to the point I can't talk when I open my mouth--only silent cries to oblivion. Some people say that it's always darkest before the dawn, but it feels like I'm stuck in the time before dawn where it doesn't get bright. I'm stuck in this darkness that's pulling me back, with an assumption that nothing is going to be perfect, but an endless hope that things will get better. And if things don't get better, I'll still make it because I always want to be a person that can help and comfort friends and family.

I like how sometimes I can forget everything and move it to the back of my mind even though it's hard. Sometimes I think about when I lived in Florida I really loved living there, but it was way too bad down there with abuse and things so I moved out. But with all of the sadness in my life there is also positivity. I'm glad that there are not only negative outcomes in my life and I'm happy that I'm able to live on this earth at all. I thank all of the people in my life, no matter what they've done with or to me. Without them, I would not be who I am today. They say it's harder to dance with the devil on your back, but I don't dance so I think I'll be fine.

LARRY, 14

When I was eight years old, my mom and dad weren't getting along. And by that I mean they just didn't like each other. They got a divorce, and there was no way they were getting back together. But they waited. When my mom moved out, my two younger sisters and my little brother kind of knew she wouldn't' be coming back, and that's exactly what happened. Ever since my mom left us, it has impacted the way I act and the way I think. Her leaving made me realize at a young age that not everything is going to be good, and not everything is going to be bad.

CHRISTIANE, 14

One battle that I had to go through is technically still happening now, but it has made me who I am. About three years ago I found out my biological father left my mom when she became pregnant with me. I had learned some stuff about him when I was six years old, because my step-sister told me that the dad I have now is not my real dad. All my mom told me at that point was that he left before I was born and that he was a bad man. I decided to look for him on Facebook, and I found him. I asked him if I could call him. He was so excited to talk to me more than I was to him. The next day I called him and we talked for several hours. I was so happy to finally talk to him and learn more about what happened. My biological father's caller ID was there for my mom to see, however. When my mom and dad got home, she saw his name on the caller ID. She called me out and asked why he called. It became the worst night of my life. I had to argue to let him call once a week-but he had to call, or there would be no call. She did this to see if he truly cared, or to prove to me that he wouldn't call and didn't care.

He called for about three months and then I received an email from him saying he didn't want to call anymore and that he doesn't really know me. The whole part of talking on the phone was to know each other, so his "reasoning" confused me. After reading the email, I called him with my mom by my side. I asked him what he meant by what he said, and it escalated into a huge argument. "I'm sick of your lies," I said. "You're a stupid twelve year old girl," he said. That was the night I started to stand up for myself in my life. I emailed him in an attempt to fix what was broken, but he continued with his lies. In the end he said, "You are a stress in my life that I don't need." When we had talked, I found out I have four half siblings. I got to know some of them and we started to develop relationships, only to have them terminated because of the constant bickering about my biological father. The one that hurt the most was when my grandpa stopped talking to me. He had promised he would never abandon me like his son did, but then he told me he no longer wanted anything to do with me. I could survive not talking to my other family members, except for my grandpa. But he up and left me too. What's weird is that I called him three months later and he didn't seem to remember saying those things to me. When I brought it up, he just got mad at me. I let it go and told him I missed him. He hasn't responded since. It's obvious something like this is going to make me have trust issues with people. It's been difficult to open up and be the nice person I used to be. I may not be proud of what I've become, but I am at the same time.

JARROD, 14

My dad left me when I was born. I thought he left because he wasn't ready to be a dad. I thought about this my whole life and kept telling myself that my mom and dad separated because of me. My mom tried making my life the best possible by working two jobs. I spent 12 to 16 hours a day in day care, five days a week. I keep thinking this is my fault because my mom and I are miserable. She has a hard time taking care of me, and the price for everything always goes up. One day, while at daycare, my mom picked me up and said, "Jarrod, today we are going to face chat your dad." I said I was okay with that, but deep down I wasn't. I didn't want to meet the man who abandoned me and my mom. When we face chatted with Jeremy (I refuse to call him Dad), it was a horrible experience. When my mom saw his new wife and their two kids, she bolted to her room and cried in her pillow. I asked Jeremy point blank, "Why did you leave my mom when I was born?" He told me he didn't want to have a child at the time and that 27 years of age was too young to have a kid. I won't even go into the logic of what the difference is between 27 and 33, when he remarried and had two kids. I didn't want to see my mom miserable anymore, so I changed my behavior and the way I live. I have been doing everything I can to take care of my mom.

JAQUELINE, 14

Divorce has always been a part of my life. But, they aren't divorced legally. They're divorced emotionally. My parents have never been in a happy relationship. There are days they tolerate each other, but days when they don't speak to each other or spend time together. They are unhappily married and only together because of me and my sisters. The first time I heard the word "divorce" was when I was seven. I came home from school that day and the skies were dark, as if ready to cry. As I approached the front porch, I could already hear my parents screaming at each other. I heard glass shattering against the hardwood floor. They had been fighting for over a week straight, but on this day I understood what they were fighting about. My mom was accusing my dad of cheating on her. Of course I didn't understand what they were talking about at that age. As soon as I walked in the screams and shattering came to a halt. Just silence. You think that was the end of it? They went right at it again and screams got louder and harsher. My mom threatened him with divorce. I started getting tense (does any seven year old deserve to feel this way?) I bawled my eyes out until I couldn't cry anymore. I stayed in my closet until my sister pulled me out. I didn't talk for hours. I will never forget that day. It shaped me and taught me how to put up an act. I feel unhappy and uneasy most days, even though people see me as "happy" and "carefree". Yeah, right. Way to put up an act, Jaqueline. I prefer to give them the version of myself that is positive, but I don't think I can show the true side of me because of the fear of my friends leaving me and calling me a liar. My friends are outgoing, but I prefer keeping to myself. I'm not happy with who I am with my friends. I'm always fake with them. I hate living a lie.

MARGARET, 14

My parents' divorce wasn't one of those "I don't love you anymore" divorces. It was more like being dragged through shards of glass, with all the heartache my dad caused. I've never been close to my dad, so the past few years have been difficult. I had been homeschooled for most of my life, but I had to transition to public school in 2012. It wasn't what I was used to, and building friendships weren't easy. Last year, seventh grade, was the worst year ever. Not only was there petty drama from everyone around me, but I also sunk into a depression. I've always had emotional problems, but last year I would come home from school, do my homework, and then sit in my room thinking myself into oblivion. I had thought about committing suicide four times a day. I lost weight before I went to the doctor and was diagnosed with severe depression and anxiety. I vowed to feel better. With a lot of hard work, some new friendships, and the strength of my teachers, 8th grade took positive shape and I'm happy as a clam.

COLLEEN, 14

Words don't describe what it's like to be told you were adopted. Millions of questions came to my mind. Who is my real mom? Where is she? My adoptive mom is my mom, however. Unfortunately, she couldn't supply me with much information because she didn't know the answers to my questions. As I got older my questions became more sophisticated, but it was more of how I viewed myself that changed. I was different in my eyes from other Asian kids that were my friends. They liked and ate so much food that is a part of their culture, but I grew up with American food so I really don't know much about my culture, other than my real name, and that my dad has a tattoo of it along with my sister's name *Fukangyan*, which means Happy Swallow. I can't get out of my head if my biological mom misses me. What does she look like? Did they have any medical conditions/history that I need to know about for my own health? Why was I put up for adoption? My parents did film a video of their journey in 2002 picking me up as an 11 month old from Fuzhou, China. I saw on the video my homeland, and what I was like. I was also able to see my foster mom crying when she handed me over to my new mom. Knowing that kind of warmed my heart, knowing she loved me, cared for me, and would miss me. I stopped asking questions, one, because my mom would get annoyed by it, and two, because I ran out of questions to ask. Instead, I told my parents I wanted to learn more about my culture. For my birthday and Christmas I get many traditional Chinese decorations, lanterns, streamers, dragons, stuffed pandas, and Chinese calendars. In 2013 my parents took me to the Chinatown part of Seattle, but I still felt like the odd one out. Everyone spoke Chinese, knew all these terms, and foods, and I knew nothing about it. So I've kinda gone full circle in being clueless as to who I am. It makes school a challenge in that I don't know my true identity and how people see me. Everyone has a different identity, looks, and interests with others, yet people who are your friends are mostly alike because they are people you get along with. All I can do is keep my head up and find the positive in things, and things will turn out for the best.

ERROL, 14

I don't remember a lot from when I was a little kid. Obviously, my parents weren't going to tell a five year old kid all of what's going on in their lives. From what I gathered, they seemed happy to me. One thing that was clear is how different they were when it came to disciplining me. They always argued about how to punish me. I was quite the little troublemaker. My parents were having marital problems when I was about seven. Arguments were frequent and over the dumbest things, but in 2009 everything came crashing down when my dad found out my mom was cheating on him. At first I was surprised, but that quickly followed with anger and then sadness. How could my mom do something so horrible? She managed to make him do something I had never seen my dad do: cry. I had always thought of my dad as a superhero that could handle anything. It was at that moment that I never wanted to see my mother again. Eventually, my mom told me her side of the story and how she regretted her choices in life. She apologized and I forgave her. My dad started dating a little while after the divorce was finalized. I have no idea how many dates he went on, but it was a few months before he introduced me to his new girlfriend. I was nervous, as was my dad. I was hoping he wasn't dating some jerk, and he was worried I would get attached with the possibility of them breaking up. Her name was Tina and she wasn't some crazy lady. My dad proposed to her a couple years later. Tina has impacted me in a positive way.

She doesn't immediately give me an answer when I ask a question. She thinks before she speaks. When I mess up, she teaches me lessons from it. She is doing what no one has done better. She is preparing me for this great big world that I will be facing in four years. While it may seem like I don't love her or want to be around her, there is a love I have for her that I have for no one else. I've heard that our character is based on 10% action and 90% reaction. With that, I believe that the events after my parents' divorce have shaped me into the person I am today.

ROBERT, 14

Divorce is so common that people assume it's no big deal. What they don't think about are the little things that make life more difficult for a teen. A lot goes into parents getting divorced. You have double the rules and double the chores. On the positive side, I get double the birthday and Christmas presents. I would say it's because of my mom that I am who I am today. She raised me and my sister all by herself. My dad is in my life, but hasn't helped my mom much. She does so much for us. Anything we need, she works hard so we can get it. She is the perfect role model. My dad does give me some advice, but there is a void because he clearly didn't know anything about us when we were younger. I was disappointed in him, but he has worked hard to help out more. Living in two houses is difficult though.

NADIE, 14

My parents divorced when I was too little to remember. All I knew was that I always went to my dad's house in Louisiana during the summer and every other Christmas. It used to be fun, until I got older. I always feel like a stranger there. Thankfully, I only have to go there for a week now. He always has a new girlfriend, and by the time I re-visit each one is gone. Sometimes I feel like he chooses his latest fling over me. He didn't even call me to tell me I was getting a new step family. Instead, he decided to text me in a group chat-not even a personal message. While I like his fiancé, I don't want to get too attached. I've made that mistake too many times. Her son is 10, and he's like every other annoying 10-year-old boy. It's hard to watch him raise other kids that aren't his, when he barely raised me. It's the little things that hurt most, like him never getting to see me do what I love. If I asked him what my favorite color is, he would fail. Some of the choices he makes hurt my feelings. When he retired from the military, he could have moved to Washington to be closer to me. Nope. He and his new family came up to see my brother graduate, but stayed in some hotel in another city instead of staying close to me. To add a cherry on top, he called me (which happens once in a blue moon) and said, "I hope we have fun up there." That may not seem hurtful, but it made me feel like I am not fun enough or good enough. My mom re-married when I was three years old. My step-dad is a good guy, and has provided me with an amazing life. But he and my mom fight a lot. It's always something. Sometimes I just want to scream, "Get a divorce!" I don't think they ever will because of my little brother. It seems like they only enjoy each other's company when they're drunk. They drink every weekend, which I hate more than anything in the world. It bothers me more than they think it does. Some people ask me why I dance and I simply say, "Because I like it." That's only partially true. I dance because it's my escape. When I'm dancing it is easy to forget my problems.

CHAPTER 9

THE NEGATIVE INFLUENCES OF OTHERS

**HARPER, 15

I am who I am because of my insecurities, my scars, and my depression. It's everything that has guided me to this point in my life. I have hated my image for years now, and even to this day I can't put it into words. But others have. They've called me the following:

*Slut

*Whore

*Cunt

*Jelly Belly

*Fat-ass

*Embarrassment

*Heartless bitch

*Attention whore

*Asshole

*Kill yourself

*I never liked you as a person

*You could lose a couple pounds

*What the fuck do you want? (insert bitchy tone)

"Oh! You're the girl that dated 8 guys in 1 week last year, right?

I've heard these words in whispers as I walk down the hallways. When I enter a room, I see the points and laughs. These words have been thrown at me so much I thought to myself: *If so many people think these things of me, then they must be true so why not go with it.*

I look in the mirror today and I see the ugliest person in the world. I recently wrote a poem about this and it read:

It's easy for you, you're pretty...

I wake up and see her. The fat slut. People think it of me, I guess it's true...

Why not embrace it..I guess it can be a part of who I am...

Her, with the stretch marks and cellulites...not good enough...

Her with the thunder thighs and flabby arms...never enough...

Her with the fat cheeks, triple chin, and shitty hair...

Her with the way she thinks she's everything...never will be...

Her with the calf's a million miles wide...cut vertical...

Her with the man hands and fat fingers...hecking hairline...

I hear the whispers...

I feel the stares...see the points...

I hear the laughs...

We Irish have a deep sadness...

I have scars on my arm and legs. They are a part of who I am and how I got here. I have to embrace it. No matter how many people tell me I'm beautiful, it doesn't do anything for me because I know that they don't know the real me. I can't please my sister, no matter what I do, I can't impress her. I let down my parents down every time I look at my grades because I know I can do better. But, I don't want to because I don't care. Last year something happened. I woke up and I couldn't get out of bed... and then it happened the next day. And it kept happening...day after day...then came me not able to go to sleep at night. All I did was lay in bed on my phone and I wasn't even tired. I'd wake up in the morning and have bags and dark circles. A couple months went by and I started to lose weight. And then I lost my appetite and more weight. I tried to tell my family about what was going on. How I'm depressed, anxious, stressed, anorexic. I tried all the time and all they would say is "You don't know what that is! You don't have any of those." They never believed me until the school counselors called and told my mom about a note I wrote to someone that I thought was my friend. What it basically said was that I was in a bad spot in my life and I was thinking about cutting again. My mom came home and she finally believed me that I needed help. I turned to stealing my parents' alcohol to deal with the pain until I got alcohol poisoning. I stopped when I realized that I didn't want that kind of life. Even to this day I hate the way I look. I wake up in the morning and get ready for the day. I start to put my makeup on and see the real me go away. I hide the real me because I care what people think of me. It's a natural thing, but sometimes it hurts knowing that people don't know the real me. Not even my parents know the real me. No one has really bothered to ask me. So I changed who I was for people to like me. I changed the way I looked, acted, everything. I care what people think of me more than I care what I think of me.

Even though I hate myself, I like where I am headed. I can lose weight without not eating, I can make friends without hiding who I am. But before people can accept *me,* I have to accept *me.*

SLOANE, 14

You would think a child would notice if her parents were on drugs. My parents are drug addicts. It shocked me when I found out because I never expected it. My parents always cared for us (my siblings) and loved us. I never thought drugs would be in the equation. The only thing that was odd was the constant flow of people coming through our door. I honestly never thought anything of it. I was used to it, I grew up with it. My parents were always locked in their room with their friends and I just saw that as private times with friends. Looking back, I am pretty fortunate for having my best friend live next door to me. I was rarely at my own home. That probably explains why I can be a bit clingy. I've always had a voice in my head telling me everyone in my life would up and leave me. By the time I was in the middle of sixth grade, my parents moved to my grandparents' house. Suddenly I had been yanked up and moved to a new school with new people. I had to start all over again making friends. I only made one friend that year, and of course with my luck, she moved away a few months later. Then my dad went in for treatment, and that intensified my clinginess 10 times. Now I'm scared I'll lose my friends. This has whirled into big depths of insecurity. Despite all this, I'm proud that I don't have to hide under a giant rock. I have enough friends that I can be myself around, and that makes me proud of who I am and who I'm becoming.

AUDREY, 13

I was nine years old when my grandmother was diagnosed with cancer. She didn't have it treated early enough, and it spread in her body. My mom would pick me up early from school nearly every day and we would visit her. I remember how much I missed going to her house before my ballet practice or when she would put my hair in a bun and occasionally do my make-up. She battled cancer for nearly a year before she kicked its butt. This taught me that there is always hope, and giving up should never be an option. She's 82 now, goes dancing, and plays Bingo. I couldn't ask for a better grandmother, and it's shaped me into being a stronger person myself.

Bernie, 13

You could say I am the one weird kid that does badly in school. Inside my head, I know I'm just lazy. I'm trying to fix it, but it's hard. I think my laziness started when I was seven years old. I was playing violent video games like Nazi Zombies from Call of Duty on my Xbox. My game playing got out of hand. I met my best friend online playing these games, and ironically, he's the one who helped me through life. He doesn't judge me, but helps me when we talk about stuff. It helps, but I still don't feel like the outside me is cool to be with, like I'm cursed to be weird forever. Here's an example of weird: The people that make fun of me are the people I hang out with. How sick is that? I also feel like I am floating away from my dad. He provides a roof over my head and we don't have money worries, but I don't seem to connect with him at all. He has all these different interests that I don't relate to. Whether it is foods, football, or even video games, we just aren't on the same page. When dinner is ready, I take my plate to my room. It's all I've ever known. My two friends are the ones that keep me going.

ALLIE, 14

The two earliest memories I have are being picked up by the cops, and being adopted. I was three years old at the time. My first family consisted of Nana and Papa. I don't know how long I was with them. Another family next door is also part of my family in that they adopted my twin sisters and triplet brothers. I grew up in a private Christian school and then was given a choice of going to public school or home school. I chose public school. I was an absolute loner. I didn't know anyone and didn't know how to socialize, so my mom started introducing me to random kids. Sure enough, these random kids became my best friends. I truly believe my friendships are what have molded me into the person I am. I did change after first grade and started building up an attitude. I dropped my "nerd" friends to "fit in". I stopped doing homework. When junior high hit, I kept to myself. I only had a few friends that let me be who I wanted to be. In 7th grade I continued not doing my homework and worried more about fitting in. As this happened, though, my attitude towards my parents changed. I got in trouble all the time. I guess it just hit me one day that my choices were impacting my friends and family. It was time for me to start figuring out who I really was. I found friends who actually liked me for me and not who I was trying to be. I'm just glad I chose a different path.

LIZBETH, 13

I am one of those kids whose parents are always fighting about something. Everything went downhill five years ago when my grandpa died. He was the "patriarch" of the family. Grandpa's house is where we would have all our parties, gatherings, and other events. He played a big role in my life; he always knew the right thing to say. He taught me a lot about cooking and animals. When he died, I realized family cannot be replaced.

Those next few months were really rough-there was a piece of our hearts that was missing, and it couldn't be filled. My whole family tried to fill that slot in different ways. I tried to fill it by playing the sport I love, fastpitch. My dad filled his spot with alcohol. When my dad drinks, he becomes furious for no reason, and some nights he would scream at me or my mom, or my brother so bad that I would just leave for the night. Thoughts of running away were always tempered when my grandpa would talk to me in my dreams. He would tell me to stay strong; that it will get better. One night my mom and dad were fighting over the fact that he should stop drinking. My dad left that night on my brother's dirt bike and hit a telephone pole and required 20 stitched from his ribs to his hip.

After that, my dad quit drinking for a while, but it didn't last very long. A couple weeks after the crash, he was back to drinking again. It had gotten so bad he had to move out. When my parents split it was very hard for me, as we kept moving houses and my grades started slipping. Three months later they finally got back together, but the fighting and screaming resumed every single night, night after night. They were back to their normal selves (sarcasm). After about a year or two my dad stopped drinking, but when he got a raise from his boss, he went out to celebrate and drank. I was so disappointed and my parents split up, again. They didn't talk for six months and I didn't see my dad this whole time. Once they started talking again things started looking up. I got to see my dad, but when I first saw him I was confused. He just walked in the house like any old dad would, and all I could do was look at him with mixed emotions of anger, confusion, fear, and happiness. Because of these tug-of-war emotions, I just turned around and walked away. I truly regret that decision, but then again, it brought me and my dad closer. We now share some of the same hobbies as my grandpa. When he died, I didn't know what to do, but, just like he said in my dreams, good things do come out of bad things.

CANDICE, 14

My dad always tried to encourage me to go to public school, but I liked private school. My aunt worked there and I loved the teachers and students I shared space with. The uniforms sucked. We had to wear white, light blue, or navy blue shirts with collars, along with khaki or navy blue pants, skirts, or dresses. By the time sixth grade rolled around, I was pretty much teaching myself because I was the only one in my grade mixed with other grades. Teachers would address the other seven kids in the class before I was taught. That's when I realized it was time for public school. I needed to go socialize with kids my own age. I was nervous about public school, but I knew I had to do this. When I stepped on the bus for the first day of junior high, my mom was a wreck. I thought about teasing her, but I was a wreck inside too. I wanted to run back on the bus when it dropped me off. Watching all these kids hugging their friends from elementary school was traumatic for me because I was alone, with no friends. Eventually, a girl sat next to me in the gym and introduced herself. Friends started to trickle after that. My nervous energy transformed into normal teenage energy. I couldn't wait to tell my family. The first person I saw was my mom. I jumped into her arms and told her about the great day. That's when I realized I can overcome any obstacle that's in my way. Social life has its drawbacks, though. The main group of friends I hang out with actually hate each other, and I'm forced to pick sides. I'm tired of them tugging me back and forth. I guess that's part of growing up.

ROCHELLE, 14

My dad has Parkinson's disease. We have always been really close. He taught me how to pitch a baseball when I was six, and we would hang out and watch basketball games on TV. Last year he was diagnosed, and life has gotten a lot tougher ever since. He was planning on retiring this coming summer from the U.S Postal Service, but bad shakes in his left arm (he is left-handed) forced him to retire early. It's so hard for him to do basic things like write, eat, and drive. The medication he takes makes him tired, so he doesn't do much anymore. I feel so helpless. I want to make him happy, but I don't know how. My mom and I argue about what we should do. We still watch basketball and sometimes throw the ball around, but I wish things could be the way they used to be. Having dealt with my family issues, it makes it easy for me to go through school. I'm kind of crazy and weird, sometimes goofy and random, but my circle of friends is accepting of one another. It bothers me when I see people pretend to be something they're not. They are lying to everyone around them and themselves just so they can be "accepted". I just make a point not to be around a fake crowd anymore. I'm not super popular and I'm okay with that. I have enough friends, get good grades, play sports, and just focus on having fun in life.

KARLEE, 14

Being shy in junior high is an experience. I sit with a couple of friends at lunch who are smart like me. But in reality, we're just the weird band kids. I feel like I have some things in common with my friends, but we're all weird and nerdy in our own unique personalities. I get along with or connect with most people, but don't get me started with annoying kids. Everyone has his or her breaking point. When I look at my friends I'd say we all have realistic outlooks on life. One misconception of being a smart kid is the idea that we must like school. While I am motivated to do well in school and want to maintain a 4.0, the truth is that I don't really like school. Yes, I am grateful for the free education and all that, but I've never gotten excited about going to school. I don't think there's anything wrong with that.

FRAN, 14

I prefer to keep to myself. I am very quiet. I have a lot of fears. I'm scared of being hurt or bullied or picked on. This has impacted me because it goes back to my elementary days when I would get bullied constantly. While it eventually stopped, I am scared it could happen again. I keep to myself so I don't have to say anything because it is my fear that I will get bullied if I say something. I am also scared of losing people because I've lost so many friends and family that I love. I hate that I am quiet around people I hang with, but I'm trapped: they could stop hanging out with me because I'm not talkative, but they could pick on me if I say something stupid. I feel I'm getting better at school because the kids here are kind for the most part. I wish so much to be fearless.

DIANE, 14

What's made me, me? While there are many things that have shaped and molded me into who I am, I feel there is one significant situation that I've experienced that impacted my life. When you think of a family, the first thing that pops into your mind is a loving married couple with a beautiful baby whom the couple will love and care for unconditionally. When I was very young, I did live with a happy, loving and caring couple, only they weren't my biological parents. I lived with my auntie and uncle while my dad served in the military. My mom had a bigger issue. She had a problem, disease, mental issue, or however else you want to label an addict. Her problems with drugs and the police are countless. She would come and go and never stay for long periods of time, but my dad still provided her with money to live on (but you can guess where that money went to). I was only two, so I didn't understand why my mom was absent. Eventually, the Navy stationed my dad in Washington State but he wasn't able to take me with him. His only option was to leave me with my aunt and uncle. Growing up with them had its pros and cons, but at the end of the day I was loved and raised by family.

At the age of four, my mom found out where I was living and she fought to gain custody of me, and we stayed in Guam. After six months of living with her, she realized she couldn't take care of me (even with my dad sending money for support). She sent me to live with my Nina (my dad's sister). At five years of age my dad gained custody of me, and I also gained a stepmom and stepsisters. My mom came to visit later and I stayed with her for a couple days, but all I remember is her shaving her hair off and selling it to support her habit. That was the last time I saw her. To this day I truly hate my mom. She chose drugs over a loving husband and a wonderful child. She has chosen a life where she never knows where she will wake up next, or maybe she'll overdose. To choose that over watching her daughter grow up and succeed is crazy. She'd rather get her fix instead of watch me win a soccer game or get an award for academics. She'd rather ask my dad for money instead of asking how I'm doing. Sometimes I have a hard time trusting people because of the amount of disappointment I've faced with my mom. I also have a hard time letting people into my life and opening up. My experiences growing up have affected who I hang out with. It wasn't until I started to accept my mom not being a part of my life that I could move on and improve myself with people. I have since made more friends and I don't have fear of being judged by others. I know as I grow and experience new things, my life is gonna change. I'll learn from mistakes, and that alone with shape me more into who I am and who I will be in the future.

NAT, 14

My whole life I've played sports, so I attribute who I am to my family and coaches mostly. I learned from them at a very young age that I had to be tough. Because I always had to be tough, I never really showed any emotion for anything except for when I was angry or happy. By not showing my emotion, I also started not talking and became the "quiet and dark" kid. I would only talk to a certain group of people because I didn't have a lot of close friends. I never wanted to be the popular kid with tons of friends because we moved a lot, and I would just get upset with starting over all the time. Now that I've lived in the same place for three years, I've been talking more and more comfortably with people. I began to show emotion again. I even cried like normal people do, but last year my dad said I wasn't allowed to cry. So now I'm back to the way I was before. Quiet and dark. Thanks dad (insert sarcasm here).

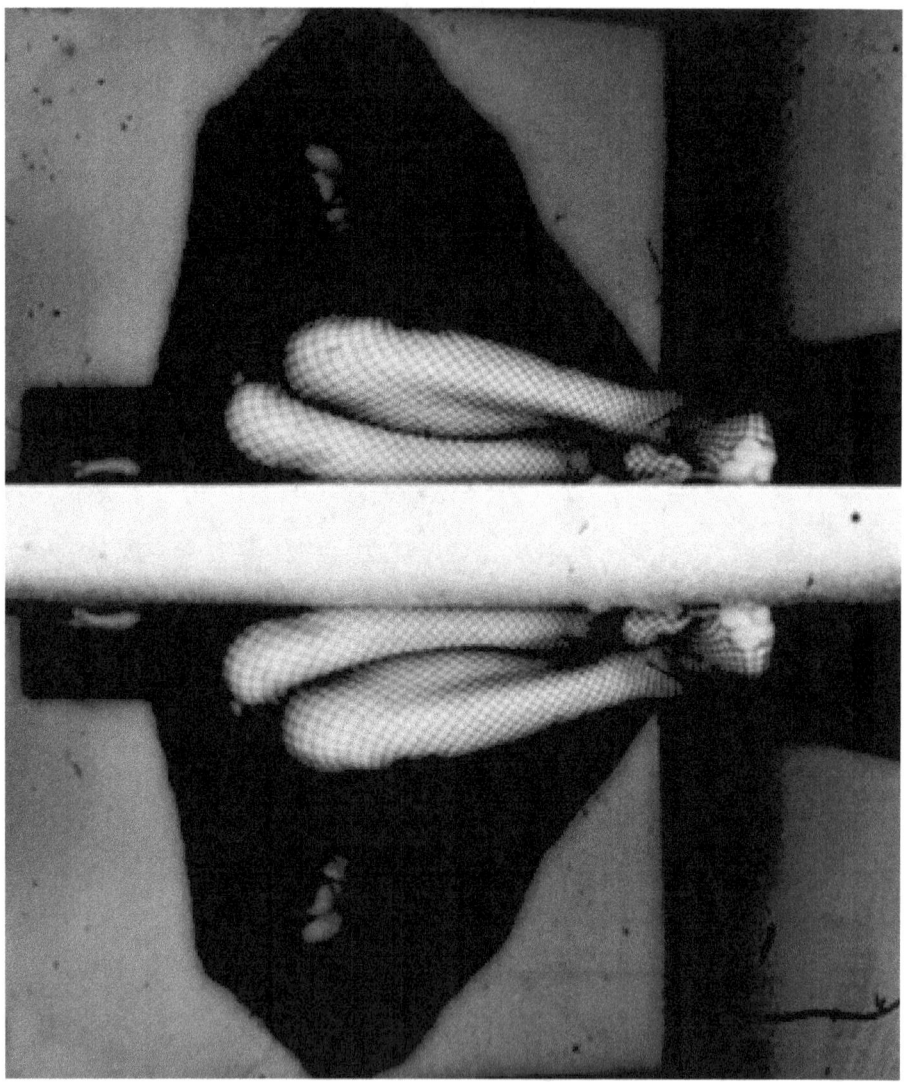

CHAPTER 10

INSECURITY/SELF-IMAGE

**CAMILLA, 14

My characteristics are like puzzle pieces. I'm really just made of blood and flesh full of alive cells. My puzzle pieces would include my step-dad, my mother, and my siblings, as well as the absence of my father. When I dig deeper, though, I see the loneliness I corrupt myself in; the self-doubt that shows so easily on my face; my inner thoughts; and my silence. I think I'm quiet because the world is dying. Society kills itself over and over by people we follow who can promise more money in our pockets. But I wonder what happens when I die? What happens when we all die? Will the pure lives float easily up to heaven and the ones who need a second chance or the one who needs to re-live life remains on earth to help in engineering, or fighting fires, saving the world, or survive the breaking down of buildings, or running away from vicious animals. I don't understand when people say the "end of the world". Yeah, the human race will die, but other life forms will continue to thrive despite our emptiness. Would that really be so bad for the human race to just die? We kill anything in sight, we take land that isn't ours, we waste food like air, and we cut trees for global demands.

Ironically, my "life" hasn't really started yet. What builds on my character may not have happened to me yet. What if that big fantastic moment of life hasn't happened? What will happen in the next five years? Maybe a terrorist attack will occur and I end up saving little kids and get labeled a hero on the newspaper lying outside your doorstep? Maybe what really defines me may not happen to me in time or it has already happened to me and I don't recognize it. It reminds me of a quote from Shakespeare. He said "Some are born great, and some achieve greatness, and some have greatness thrust upon them." Maybe that is true, but maybe half of the people don't achieve anything and just sit at home lost in their own minds. Maybe you'll see me doing something with my life, living it to the fullest with one thing that defines me, many things, or nothing.

**KATHLEEN, 13

I have been judged, backstabbed, heartbroken, happy, filled with joy, and throw a little crazy in there and it's a never-ending life cycle. Each day feels like a new chapter, with each element adding a highlight to my memories. And I am sharing it all with you.

My mom has always told me that I am a miracle. That I wasn't supposed to be here. That I am a gift. She wasn't supposed to have a child, as told by many doctors. They called her an infertile turtle. But one day she met my dad and the miracle happened. The miracle wasn't just the Immaculate Conception. When I was born, I wasn't breathing because my umbilical cord wrapped around my neck. I was rushed away and my mom couldn't see me til the next morning, when I was cleared of any further health issues.

I am grateful for being here, and my friend's 3-year-old sister at the time is too. When I was nine years old I saved her life. I was pushing her on a swing and she was getting really high. Underneath the swing was a black rubber mat. My foot caught on the mat and I ended up knocking her over. She started to fall, but I caught her on my chest and hands before she bounced on the ground. I remember that day like it was yesterday.

Speaking of bouncing, I've seesawed between Alaska, Washington, and Oregon over the last five years. It was my last move to Seward, Alaska when my life went to hell. It started when I stopped sitting with "popular" kids because I preferred the other kids. As a result of this choice, people were told not to sit next to me. They called me "bitch", "whore", "slut", and I was told to "kill myself" all in the first two weeks of school. I came from being grateful for my life to this. I wasn't prepared to feel this way and it scared me. I went home every day crying and my mom asked me what was wrong, but I just closed slammed the door in her face and told her to leave me alone. Add the inner anguish of my dad coming up to visit with his new wife, who I didn't want to see, put me in a bad way. But, when he showed up I started to cry a little since I hadn't seen him in eight years. We went out to eat and he barely talked to me. But his wife talked to me and I ended up liking her.

A month later, a sigh of relief came over me when we moved to another town in Alaska (closer to where my dad lives). I could put the past behind me and forget about Seward. Life was going well, but then I was uprooted earlier this year and told we had to move back to Washington to deal with stuff. I find myself hiding who I am more here than Alaska, but I am still the same person. I am just excited to add new chapters to my life.

DELANEY, 13

Have you ever paid attention to how you act? Have you ever acted like a different person, or do you act like yourself? Me? I act like an alternate person all the time. I am a fake person. I am a foster kid and for the past few months I've been completely different at home from school. I've been having a few nervous breakdowns, yet I keep them for myself. When you realize how tough life is as a foster kid, you start to understand why they put a mask on to hide everything. I had a mask on all year this year. I started hiding everything and never talked to people about my problems because I don't want any sympathy. I don't care what people say or think about me because putting me down isn't going to work. I will stand up to defend myself no matter what situation I'm in. For the past seven years I've been raised by a foster family that is always busy working, and we never stop. I guess this had developed my pride and determination that is within me. Yeah, a lot of stuff has happened in my life. I wear the mask at home because I don't want my foster mom to know what's in my head. This is my life now and I'm not going to let people treat me like trash or bring me down anymore.

**DEBORA, 14

At 11 years of age I was diagnosed with severe depression. I always knew there was something different about me. I was never truly happy and everything I enjoyed soon became boring or uninteresting. I secluded from other people, became quiet, and didn't speak in class. I didn't have many friends and only one or two really talked to me. My illness made it hard for me to be motivated, even to get out of bed.

My anxiety issues made for a lethal combination with my depression. I would get panic attacks randomly even if nothing triggered it. I became discouraged. When I started junior high, it was my fifth school already. I stayed quiet, but it didn't stop people from talking about me. I was hated for no reason. I cut off any of my friends I had left because I didn't want to pull them into the mess I call my life. The only person I had was my mom. I was getting bullied and sexually harassed. Even after enrolling in an online school, I couldn't shake what I was told, and I started to think they were right about me. The counselors at the school said I should just brush it off because "this kind of thing happened all the time". So I never spoke up again and unhappiness wrapped my entire body. No one knew what was going on with me. I acted like everything was okay. I acted happy and laughed. I simply put on a mask for everyone. I didn't feel accepted unless I acted a certain way. My only outlet has been music. It is my escape. It's helped me through bullying, all the moving I've done, and the illnesses that haunted me.

It doesn't help having a disconnected family. My dad doesn't care about me and my mom had a child with her boyfriend when I was seven. I have always felt like they loved my baby brother more than me. I had always been an only child and then he was born on top of inheriting a stepsister from my mom's boyfriend. Then I found out my biological father had two other daughters.

Moving so often caused me to distance myself from people because I knew I'd just end up leaving again. And then the worst happened. My mother left. How can I trust anyone now? All these issues changed a girl who once used to be outgoing, happy, and adventurous and churned me into someone who wants to hide from everyone. I am still adventurous in that I like the outdoors and it's a way to calm me and make me feel better. But essentially, I'm the quiet girl in the back, with colorful hair who no one really knows.

DAVID, 14

I don't think I know who I am yet. I've gone through so much early in my life that the only thing I can say it's done for me is give me a thick skin. My parents got divorced when I was young, my dad lost everything, committed a crime, and went to prison. I haven't seen him since. It's hard to explain my life. I lost my parents, lost a dog that I loved, and got bullied in school. I moved to Washington State with my aunt (my legal guardian) a few years ago and life's been a little more normal. My aunt is my hero. She bought two dogs and a calm place for me to live. If I learned anything from my young life, it's that I couldn't control who made me who I am. School seems foreign to me socially. I dress decent and kinda act cool, but that's not who I am. I act fake to get around with my friends. I will say funny things to look cool. I'm not comfortable when I act this way. I guess the only way I can get people to like me is to act fake. There's the tradeoff. I'm never disliked by anyone, but then I can't act myself. I guess there's nothing wrong with being funny and friendly.

CECILY, 14

I never believed I would make friends that would understand what I go through. I mean, it was school and almost everyone is fake. And the ones who weren't fake were the ones being made fun of. Naturally, I tried to blend in and listen to the same popular music others listen to despite not being a fan of the music. I wanted to fit in. It wasn't until sixth period class I sat next to a girl that seemed genuine to me. She wore skinny jeans and an oversized sweatshirt. "Hi, I'm Jane," she said as she faced me with a bright smile. I looked closer at her and she had a ton of freckles all over her face. "Hi, I'm Cecily," I said. And then we sat in awkward silence until the teacher came in. "Hi. I'm Mr. Kranz. Pair up," he said. I eyed her and she eyed me and we were instant partners in crime. We have helped each other out with our struggles and we've worked on fixing each other's bad habits. She changed my life and showed me the best in kids. Deep down, I feel that we all have goodness. She has made me a happier person. I've also made friends that, just like me, don't care what others around them think. My friends are very forward and real. I'm proud to say that people at my school know me for who I am and not what they want me to be or become.

CALLA, 14

I am many things, attributes, and traits, but I have had the most experience with insecurity. Various, and by various I mean hundreds, of circumstances have shaped me to be insanely insecure. Insecurity can lead to many pitfalls, but in my life, it's led to none other than an enormous waste of time, anxiety, stress, and missed opportunities, and all because I believed and cared too much about what people thought about me. My first extreme insecurity, which still haunts me to this very day, started in first grade. It was during music class, everyone had to take it. One day, my class and I were singing a song and our teacher was walking around listening, just listening. She stopped next to me, heard me sing, and then she said "You should practice singing more, like in the shower." and she made the motion of scrubbing her arms and underarms. Even though everyone I have told says she could've meant something else, I still don't believe them, and I haven't sung in front of anyone since. In 2nd grade my best friend told me I had hairy arms. She didn't mean harm by it, she was just noticing it. I got embarrassed immediately, and for the rest of that school year and two more, I did everything possible to avoid showing my arms in public, wearing long sleeve sweaters and shirts every day.

I remember I used to go to mirrors and back away to see how far away people could see it.

One of my small, but lifelong insecurities was about my eyes. My whole life people have told me it looks like I got punched in both eyes, because they have really dark circles. This hasn't affected me as much as other incidents, but has made me self-conscious enough to buy makeup to hide it. As you can see, I've only listed a few of the million unfortunate events that have happened to me throughout my life.

These things still happen, and I do still get insecure. Everyone does. But the difference is, now I'm trying my best not to hide them, and to not become as obsessed as I was before with hiding, or concealing, or burying them.

ANASTASIA, 14

Before I started public school in fourth grade, my family was being tormented and abused by my dad. After 16 years of marriage, my mom got a divorce. As a child I was happy and joyful despite the abuse, and just thought it was normal. But I didn't know that it wasn't normal for everyone to be "punished" like I had been. I started to change in fourth grade when I saw teachers and other peoples' families actually being "family". I realized my past wasn't normal. The following year I started to feel the pressures that come with public school. I didn't think I was pretty enough thus becoming quiet and shy because of my insecurities. Education was also a struggle because I was slow in math, reading, and writing. To this day I always have to work harder than most to keep up. School took its toll on me and in 7th grade I sunk into a depression, feeling lost as to who I was and what I wanted to do with my life. 8th grade became my best year as I got help from my family and I developed a relationship with Jesus Christ. I was faced with a choice: Do I let depression and anxiety control me, or do I accept myself and strive to get better? I chose the latter. I'm still quiet and shy. I am only my true self with my family. I feel like I have to be different around people at school because I don't want to feel rejection or embarrassment. I want to fit in, but at the same time I am at war with myself to be myself at school. Do I risk people not liking me, or should I be somebody everyone wants to be around? At home, I am loud and outgoing, funny, and positive. So why can't I be like this at school? It's a daily struggle at school, as I feel sad that nobody truly knows who I am. No one knows that I do love myself, and that I'm positive. Instead, I'm the insecure, shy girl that I have to hate.

TIANI, 14

Up until now, I never thought about how I became who I am today. I never thought about why I have trust issues, body image issues, and why I prefer being with adults instead of people my own age. I grew up without my dad around much because of work. My mom and grandparents took care of me the first four years of my life. Because of my father's coming and going, I thought that when he would leave he would never come back. This must be the source of my trust issues. In my own image I'm an overweight girl. I wish I didn't see myself this way. When my mom was in high school, she was a size 2, but after I was born she sprouted to a size 26. She got surgery to rid the weight, but something went wrong and she had to have a second surgery to fix the first one. She still lives with those complications today. When I see pictures of my mom in high school, I see someone I wish I could be. When I see pictures of models, I want to be them. I want the attention they get. I'm also an only child. This, on top of growing up without other people my age, is the reason I prefer adults. Ironically, when I'm with adults I am the shy, quiet kid that hides in a corner with animals. At school, I'm a whole different person. I laugh, go out of my way to help people, and try to be with my classmates as much as possible. I am more myself at school, yet I prefer being with adults more. I try to be this perfect teenager who has her whole life planned out, but when I'm at school I can be who I really am.

CHAR, 14

When I was little I used to be that kid who didn't care about my body shape, flaws, and imperfections. But that has changed as I am becoming a teenager dealing with emotions, low self-confidence, and insecurities. I have been questioning myself, "Is this the real me?" During the middle of 5th grade, one of my "friends" decided to call me fat. That was the day when I cried all the way home and lied to my mom that I fell. After that day, I have been insecure about my weight and how I looked. I didn't do anything at the time since I was only 11, so I just wore big baggy clothes so people won't notice my fat ugly body. In sixth grade my family and I moved from San Diego because my dad is in the Navy. Simultaneously, I only had a few close friends. I remember one day my friends and I made a group chat on iMessage. We talked about our insecurities and found out that we were all insecure about our body shapes. We reached a consensus decision that night we were going to go on a diet, losing at least 2 pounds. I remember the next day after we talked about our insecurities, my friends brought salads from home while I was in the lunch line buying pizza. I felt miserable and fat eating right in front of my friends, but I had nothing else to eat. Our diet didn't last more than a day and we ended up eating normal food.

The summer going into 7th grade was the worst time of my life. I immediately thought about my body. I looked at myself through a mirror and called myself fat and ugly. I also stared at my humongous thighs, and no thigh gap. I came to a conclusion that the only thing that will make me happy is to have a thigh gap. That was the time I skipped meals/starved. I remembered one day, the only thing I ate was one small bite of an apple. I also remembered that every time I would leave my house I would always look at my thighs before we headed out. 7th grade was about to start and I could see my thigh gap starting to form. Every morning my mom would always tell me, "breakfast is the most important meal of the day," before I head out the bus stop. I told her I would eat breakfast at school, which I did not. I would eat lunch at school, but not that much, and once in a while I would eat dinner. This was my cycle all of 7th grade.

In the end of 7th grade, I was skinny and I had a thigh gap, and achieved the body I wanted during the summer. I was underweight, but now recovering from my mistakes and slowing building up my confidence. I realized that I didn't need to be skinny or have a thigh gap to be perfect. I accepted the fact that everyone, including me, has insecurities and flaws. I now understand how important it is to love yourself, and to accept who you are.

DAISY, 14

Growing up I was always a weird, happy kid. Nothing could get me down. I was like kryptonite for feeling sad. I was also a very mature kid for my age. I knew of all the bad in the world before first grade, but even then I still saw the good in the world… until I was seven years old, when I stopped seeing the good in the world. I started seeing the difference between me and my much skinnier friends. No one really bullied me about it until I was older, but then, in second grade something just clicked in my head telling me that I am fat and that I will never truly be friends with the skinny girls because they saw what I saw in myself. After years of constantly putting myself down about my weight, my family decided to take me to the doctors where they not only told me I was obese but that the sadness I was feeling was because of depression. The heavy weight was simply a link to my depression. This hit my family hard. My parents started to constantly fight about me, trying to figure out someone to blame, when in reality it was my fault and the fighting didn't help. I decided to wear a mask around all my family and friends and communicate with them that "everything is fine" or "I am so happy". The mask fit so well, I started to believe I was actually happy. Compound that with my parents' belief that I was too young to be drugged up on medication, and my dislike of doctors because of the constant feeling of being judged, and it's amazing to me I didn't break down. The love I had for my grandpa was the only thing that truly made me happy. When he got sicker and sicker it hit me like a ton of bricks. I still remember playing with the model trains out in his garage laughing and playing as we made up nice lives for the little people in our pretend city going to work on the train, having a perfect life. Since he got sick we couldn't do that anymore, he couldn't even walk anymore. This is when I finally took off my mask, but that meant I emotionally shut down and spent all day and night in my bedroom other than seeing my grandfather in the hospital. When most people think of depression, they think of suicide or cutting yourself, so after a while that's what I started to think about too. Thoughts usually lead to actions. I never cried when cutting myself. It was kind of weird because after so long of being numb I started to feel something. Although it was the pain I felt, it started making me feel other things like happiness. It was like a medicine. But the more I did it in order to feel the emotions of happiness, the less it made me feel happy, and the more depressed I got. It got to the point where I wasn't even feeling the pain of the cuts on my skin. One day I cut too deep and I could see blood leaving my body. I was still numb. I just closed my eyes and gave up. Two days later, I woke up in the hospital to my mother crying in the corner wondering how she didn't notice that I was this unhappy. After a while of sitting there comforting my mother, I realized that I almost died. I decided then I would never cut or attempt to kill myself ever again. My doctor prescribed four different medications for my depression. I found it amazing how taking pills could make me so happy. This time, with the help of the medication, I could take my mask off and still be happy. I didn't need that stupid mask anymore. Everything was going well until my grandpa eventually died.

While it hit me so hard, I didn't shut down like the old me would have. I just stood there thinking about it and processing it. To this day I still haven't cried about it. I find it funny when my peers look at me when they think of someone who is always happy or is chill. They don't know the pain I went through to get here. They don't know the pills I take to stabilize myself. And they won't, because they'd never understand.

I have the urge to be who I used to be before I was seven years old. The love and support of my family, mixed with the pills I take every day to keep my depression in check aren't the only things that make me, me, but those are the things that allow me to push away my demons and let me be the happy, weird kid I am today.

CADENCE, 13

If I could travel back in time, I would do it in a heartbeat. Because of being surrounded by the wrong crowd and being influenced negatively, I can't wear shorts or shirts that show my stomach, because of all the scars that surround my body. I couldn't even enjoy volleyball back in the beginning of eighth grade without even being asked, "What's that on your leg?" and having to quit at the end. I have to wear spandex or have to constantly pull down my shorts during Track and Field this year because I was ashamed of what was painted on my leg. In sixth grade, I felt like I was being choked. I started cutting myself because a bunch of friends and I started to starve to be skinnier. People asked me if I was okay, but every time I pretended. I never was happy. It gave me and my parents stress because I began acting angry and overly confused. At the end of the year, I was about fifty or sixty pounds and having a thigh/thin gap. I also began to be violent. I would kick people in the back, or throw a basketball away from its destination. I even embarrassed one of my best guy friends by making him walk away with a red face; only because I thought it was funny. Seventh grade was when I met people that made me constantly question my life choices. I did the eraser challenge with two other friends, meaning we literally erased the skin off of our body. I started eating, but I was around the sixty or seventy pound range. I began ditching fourth period every now and then, started swearing, and got into cyber/school fights because of the word, "fake". All of us stopped talking to each other, but they still trash-talk about me to this day. I couldn't take this lifestyle anymore, so I cut myself with a pencil sharpener razor. I couldn't take my parents telling me to "suck it up" because I just couldn't do it. The longer I held in my problems, the more it felt as if it was paralyzing me on the inside. In eighth grade, I felt fake. And I began to be careless with my weight and my life. I even joined sports to try and be accepted. That didn't help either. I am still haunted by a moment during a road basketball game. The home crowd screamed, "3… 2… 1…" when there were 12 seconds on the game clock; I shot the ball prematurely and everyone started laughing. When I got home, I cried myself to sleep without feeding myself since I was so embarrassed. My parents told me to try harder in school since my grades were B's. But I couldn't, I wasn't like my siblings or someone my parents would be proud of… I hated that.

I didn't want to live beyond that point, I already screwed up my life already. I've done things I shouldn't have done, including fighting with my parents to the point where I couldn't call them "Mom" or "Dad" and they couldn't call me their daughter anymore. What kills me inside is that my parents don't trust me anymore because of what I've done to them and myself. I couldn't run away anymore. I was stressed and broken, so I cut myself again. Two months later, I'm still not happy with who I am yet, and I'm still disappointed in the way I was shaped today. I'm two months clean of cutting and maintaining a not-very-healthy weight of 96 pounds; I also learned a lesson I'm going to hold on for many years: If a psychologist holds a glass in front of you and asks, "How heavy is this glass of water?" The question itself doesn't matter, but what does matter is how long you hold onto the glass. Holding the glass for one minute doesn't hurt a lot; for an hour your arm would start to tingle. Maybe you'll begin to feel weak but there's still strength holding the glass up. But holding the glass for more than an hour, your arm feels paralyzed and numb; you just can't feel your arm anymore. That's just like stress or depression. The longer you keep whatever is weighing you down inside, the more paralyzed and weak you feel. So today, I've opened myself to feelings again. I have finally begun hanging with the right crowd, and I'm back being the girl I used to be before sixth grade.

JEMMA, 13

As a child, I never really had much confidence, and I had many insecurities. In 5th grade, I was a talkative girl with only a few friends. One night my friend had an argument over the Internet with this girl in our class. She had very rude comments to say, and my first thought was to stick up for my friend. Shortly after, I turned my phone on to see rude things said about me. It listed all my insecurities from how I act to how I looked. It's crazy to think that a 5th grader could say such cruel things. After that I never talked to my friends anymore, and I'd cry every night thinking about why I'm so worthless and annoying. They'd say things like, "you're not the same anymore," or, "why are you ignoring me?"

A year after, I moved to Washington. But, unlike living physical beings forever, words from the past follow you forever. I became friends with lots of people in 6th grade, but we all drifted apart, and I could feel my confidence fading. Whether it was my acne or comparing myself to others, I just wasn't content with how I looked and who I was.

Going into junior high as a 7th grader was kind of rough because I didn't have any classes with half of my friends, and I was not very social. I wouldn't know who to sit by at lunch. I'd walk around and sit at random tables. By the end of the year I made many friends, but I still wasn't confident, and I had a new insecurity-my weight. I started to lessen my food quantities. I'd constantly check my weight and I started to notice my weight dropping. It wasn't low enough so I'd only eat a few snacks every day.

This past year in 8th grade is when I finally snapped out of it and had some realizations. I immediately stopped skipping meals, because it wasn't healthy. I became more social, and my insecurities were slowly going away-my confidence was on the rise. I was back to being a bubbly and talkative girl. I have the most amazing friends and I have accepted the fact that everyone including myself has perfect imperfections.

ARLETTE, 14

For the people who know me, they never would've guessed that I am the person I am because of my experiences. Everyone seems to have one event that turned or changed their view on life. I haven't... yet. But I do have all this luggage I carry with me that made an impact. Life is different when it comes from two contrasting perspectives. My Asian mother was raised in a culture where she called one room huts as homes, and her biggest concern was when she would get her next meal. My white father was your typical all-star athlete, 4.0 GPA, and always went somewhere exotic over summer break. Growing up, it was almost had if someone cut me in half and glued those two sides together. I knew that in this generation this situation wasn't uncommon, but I would've never imagined that it would be a significant part of who I am today. As a kid, people could tell I wasn't average. I was bright, kind, and had a promising future. I refused to follow the people around me, until a boy put the words "ugly" and "worthless" in my head. I know that I'm better than that, but words like that stick to you for a very long time. The world began to influence me greatly, as well as my actions. I used to be so careless and free, but it was spinning so rapidly out of control. By third grade I hated to look in a mirror because I feared that

I wouldn't like what I saw. The following year, my mom announced to me that she was sick with kidney disease, and that we were expecting another kid. One event I always remember is when I walked into my 4th grade teacher's room and heard the phrase, "That's your mom?" I knew I did not look at all like my parents, but everything I knew to be stable was slowly falling apart, especially when she gave birth to my younger sister and started to get sicker. She told me that doctors originally diagnosed her with kidney disease after I was born. I carry that guilt with me forever. She always told me that it was never my fault. Bullshit. To cover up my instability, I started to wear trendier clothes, became more social, and kept my grades up as high as possible. I couldn't let my parents know how I was really feeling, so I put my feelings to the side. Having a mom who didn't understand that a boy turning you down was practically the end of the world when you're 12 made me insecure. My father, meanwhile, may not be female, but he sure did understand things like this better. I concentrated on other things like music and my studies, and I started to become more athletic to keep me busy so I wouldn't focus on what was happening around me. Being the oldest, you are expected to have everything together and never ever be wrong. I eventually worked my way to the top. When I mean top, I mean I was finally in the group considered "popular". I didn't want the circumstances to influence who I was in a bad way. I thought I was "rising" against it, but I didn't want people's sympathy. If I was considered popular no one would ever assume that anything was wrong with me. That's what I wanted. Suddenly, life took another a sharp turn as soon as I escaped elementary school. I was earning a label of a "goody-goody", while my mom became sicker than ever. On top of that, I had to deal with the prowess of my "younger" older sister, who was working her ass off to become the best she possibly could at basketball and fastpitch while transforming into an over-dramatic diva. On top of that, my dad was focusing on earning his Master's degree. This may not seem like much, but being only in 7th grade and coming home to empty house too many times to count wore on me. The countless notes and voicemails left for me was too much to tolerate, so I immersed myself in activities. It didn't change anything. It only allowed me to avoid what I was feeling until I would go into my room and just cry. Nobody knew what was going on with me. I didn't know what was going on with myself. Yeah, I knew I was very fortunate to have a roof over my head and parents that love me, but I wasn't happy. This sadness soon turned into anger. I never got my parents' attention. They always focused on my younger sisters, and assumed that I had it "together". I started to inflict all of this pain on myself. I wasn't necessarily suicidal-just angry. I was careful, however, going to school like nothing ever happened because I never wanted attention like that. I had a reputation of someone who was always happy, balanced and caring. But, on the inside I was suffering from low self-esteem and depression. People always assumed that someone like me is confident in everything I do. Truth is I hate a lot of things about me. I don't consider myself that attractive, I hate my figure, and I especially hate how people have recently labeled me as "emotionless." I was truly only average at every activity I participated in. I was okay at acting, an okay musician, okay athlete, and okay daughter. I can honestly say that the people who I was friends with growing up influenced who I was in a good and bad way. I have become more of myself this year, despite carrying so much. I always had the phrase, "people have it worse than you" in the back of my head. But, that doesn't make anyone feel better. This has been my biggest struggle. When you are a teenager, you are never fully confident in anything, and your biggest worry is what people think of you. I still think that deep inside I am still that bright, happy, carefree girl. And maybe that's who I will be 10 years from now. I know I'm headed towards a successful future because even though, my parents didn't pay much attention to me growing up, I always was on the honor roll and my teachers pushed me to be well rounded in every subject. That's pretty much it. The biggest advice I can give is to never underestimate someone's smile. There's always a deeper story behind it.

CHAPTER 11

WHAT'S IMPORTANT

** VIV, 14

Cancer can change a person and impact their life along with their family. I was five years-old when we found out my mom had breast cancer. I remember my mom trying to explain to my three year-old brother what was going to happen to her. I remember her saying "they're going get all of the bad things out of me."

In a 3-year-old's mind with Halloween on the brain he responded with, "like carving a pumpkin? How you take all the insides out before you carve it?"

"Yes, like a pumpkin!" My mom replied. That was my earliest memory of cancer in my life. I remember my mom laying on the couch when we got home from school or the many hospital visits to my mom. Walking through the door with my hand in my dad's hand and seeing my mom lying on the hospital bed, the quietness of the room and the beeping of the machines. I remember all the times we stayed at a friend's house while my dad spent the night with my mom at the hospital or my dad was at work supporting our family.

When my mom had cancer it changed my life, I became happier and respected my life more. I realized that I had almost lost my mom. A few years later my grandma was diagnosed with cancer. I was very close to her, she passed away when I was about 10 years-old.

The summer of my 8th grade year my mom was diagnosed with cancer, again. At the time, my mom was going to school to become a teacher. Even though my mom had cancer and will have cancer for the rest of her life, she still is working hard to become a teacher.

My mother has inspired me to do my best even when times get tough. Cancer may limit you, but that doesn't mean you just give up. My mother lives a daily life and still manages to take care of my family, go to school, have time for family time and juggle all of her appointments. My mother is my role model, my super hero, and the greatest mother I could ever ask for. I don't know what life would be like if I didn't have my mother in my life.

ABILENE, 13

My family is very supportive of me and has helped shape who I am today. My family has always pushed me, encouraged me, and supported me. There's been times where I haven't wanted to do something or thought I couldn't do something, but my family pushed me to do it. My dad has inspired me to do my best and take nothing for granted. When he was growing up, he didn't have a stable family or home. Ever since I was born, I've had a stable family and home. I've learned to appreciate what I have and not take anything for granted. I'm lucky enough to have parents who care, a supportive brother, and loving grandparents. I live in a nice house, good community, and great friends. My dad wasn't lucky enough to have all of those things that I have. Knowing that, and understanding what I have, has made me appreciate everything I have.

Along with everything my dad has taught me about being appreciative, my friends and neighbors have helped make me who I am. My neighbors have been my best friends since I was two years old, and they have made a huge impact on who I am today. I know for sure that I would not be the athlete that I am today without my neighbors. As a 7th grader there would have been no chance that I would have been looked at for varsity basketball, let alone starting. They played basketball with me every night for years. Not only have they helped me develop into the basketball player that I am, they helped me become a better soccer player as well. They would play soccer with me for hours a night. I am lucky enough to have my best friends live across the street from me in a cul-de-sac with multiple basketball hoops and big yards. That's where I honed my athletic ability and skill.

My parents also started me a year early in kindergarten at the age of four. It has forced me to play up to my competition and interact with older kids. I'm thankful for this, as it has made me a better student and athlete. Since I am a year younger in my grade, I get the opportunity to play with kids that I wouldn't normally interact with or know in sports because athletic teams are usually set up by age, not grade. I think that who I am is pretty similar to the people I hang out with. Most of my friends are as fortunate as I am to have a loving family and stable home-life. Many of my peers have seen their parents' marriages dissolve or other things happen in their life that have impacted them, but overall I think most of the people I am closest with share similar backgrounds and lifestyles as me.

I am happy with who I am as a junior high student. I am proud of myself for what I have accomplished before and during junior high. I am glad that I have had all of the opportunities that I have, and all of the accomplishments that come with it.

**OLIVER, 14

I put smiles on peoples' faces every day and inspire others to do more than they're expected. I think we all should ask ourselves if we are living the life we want to live. Then follow that path to success. If you don't, then you're just sitting there thinking instead of doing what you should improve instead of doing. Life can be difficult but you need to learn from experiences and suck it up and deal with it.

Have you ever had a person in your life one day and dead the next? I have and it is a horrible experience to go through. The very next day when you wake up, you sit on your bed replaying that horrible fresh memory and it sticks with you forever. And when you think about the funeral, it means that you cared about that person who just died. And when you care, you make a difference for yourself.

Have you ever seen a homeless person on the side of the road with a sign? I can't imagine how many people walk past that person without a care in the world. I don't have money to give, but I would provide food so he cannot starve.

One day in your life you're going to be in deep doo doo. I stabbed my brother in the arm accidently. To this day I feel bad about it and bad memories stick to you like a leech in a swamp...but so do good memories.

I have also had experiences with lying and peer pressure that have led to consequences I'm not proud of. But I've become a better person because of it. What's really on my mind though is the concept of "cool kids". "Cool kids" are not technically "cool". They are just wannabes. The reality is there are more uncool kids then cool kids. "Cool" boys think of themselves as stronger, faster, and better looking than others. "Cool" girls think other girls are ugly, and not popular. What kids don't think about is the future. The future I see with these so called cool kids is no different than the other kids. They will soon hit the adult workforce and they won't choose who their co-workers. But the best workers are ones that have learned to accept and appreciate others that do a great job. I'm not seeing a lot of "praise" in the schools. At least I know I'll be valued in the adult world.

FINN, 14

I choose my friends wisely and carefully. I know a lot of people, but I don't call them my friends. My friends will help me if I need it and I will help them. Almost all of them play sports and have good grades. My grades fluctuate between A's or B's, with an occasional C. My cousins, who are three and five years old, changed me by teaching me to be more careful of my surroundings. They are amazing and love to play outside with me and my brother. Whenever we go outside I'm the one in charge of them and where they go.

My mom has influenced me, making me be more independent by doing my own chores such as the dishes and laundry. My dad has taught me to plan things out more. I have more of a schedule when I stay at my dad's. Some of my friends' parents are divorced and I have seen how that has impacted them negatively, but when my parents divorced, my personality never changed.

Having pets changed me too. They taught me how to be more responsible and careful. I think of these things in my upbringing has allowed me to develop a hard shell that makes it difficult for someone to make me mad. I only get mad if something happens to a family member or friend. I credit my grandparents for instilling in me the will to save money. I have a system where three quarters of my earnings is saved and one quarter I spend. I think that was part of teaching me not to be greedy and avoid wasting money.

At school I don't fake things or hide. I am just me. I make sure I separate school from home. I don't like to bring stuff from home to school or school to home. I like to make everybody's life as easy as possible by doing my job and help whenever I can. I do get embarrassed easily on certain things though. One thing that embarrasses me easily is being with people who are not properly dressed for the occasion. If somebody is wearing basketball shorts and a tank top to a wedding I am not going to hang out him; I will act like I do not know him. If I want to go to Walmart and the person I'm with is wearing pajamas or something that's not for public, I'm not going in with him.

I'm always trying to make sure my brother gets his work and chores done on time. I'm pretty much Darry, the responsible older brother from The Outsiders and my brother is Ponyboy. Sometimes I am too rough with my brother and he gets hurt. But most of the time when I ask him to do something he will do it. I just don't want my brother to get bad habits and not do well in school or at home.

In sports I try to look at the people who are better than me and try to figure out what their techniques are and how they do it. I did track and field and the people who beat me in the hurdles and looked at their form and I tried to mimic them. Sometimes it worked but sometimes it failed.

Some people call me respectful and I like to think I am too. A lot of people can trust me with things to hold and to get stuff done. Some people even trust me with money. I don't like to let people down or make them not like me unless they're mean or don't deserve respect at all.

MAGGIE, 13

It's really hard to pick things that have shaped who I am. It's countless. I think my biggest issues is the constant judgment I face for literally everything I do. Getting called "fat", "slut", "ho", has impacted me. Nobody likes to be called names but it has made me stronger. It's taught me that even when I didn't want to live that I needed to. It showed me that the people that say those things to me and try to bring me down aren't worth my time. I'm better than that and I have a purpose. Lesson one is that I don't care to impress anyone to be who they want me to be. I do what I want for me. I would sink into such a sadness in the past until I loved myself and realized it meant nothing. I like who I am and I'm not the things people have called me. When they judge me they do not define me. They are defining themselves. I realized there's no fighting negative comments because someone will always talk about me and question who I am. I just have to smile and do what I want to do because that is what's best for me.

TINA, 14

When I started 4th grade in Oklahoma I was only 10 because I was held back in kindergarten. Back then I was a nothing. I had no personality. I didn't talk to anyone. I only cared about my grades and all I ever did was read a book to pass time. I didn't really even read them, more like skimmed the words and they would go in my head and out my ears. I didn't even care what I was reading as long as I had something to look at. I didn't have any friends and didn't question why, but I know why now. I didn't feel anything. I didn't care if kids avoided me. As long as my grades were good, my life was fine. I was able to watch TV and play on the computer as long as my schoolwork was done, however, they were concerned about my social well-being and tried to get me to be more open with others. I didn't know what they meant. What was there to open up about? I always thought the way I was, was what I was supposed to be. I kept to myself, I did my work ahead of time, and I wasn't mean to anyone in class. While most kids can claim life changing experiences from choices and events that involve other people, it was a book that shaped me and changed my life. Amazing how one little book could have that kind of effect on me. They way everything seemed to move and talk so magically was amazing. The emotion I felt inside as I read was warm and flowing. Then I started acting like the characters in the book. It was through this I started to mold a personality. I was still quiet, but was kind to everyone. I realized my purpose on earth was to be an Otaku. That is Japanese for being overly obsessed with a hobby that revolves around manga or anime. For me it's romance anime. I can't go a day without reading something romantic in the least. Japanese culture seems to just call to me wherever I go. But my life isn't all sunshine and rainbows. I had to grow up faster then I should have in Oklahoma because of something that happened to me. It's too private to discuss, but I found manga and now that I live in Washington State I feel like I'm a full vibrant person.

STEPHANIE, 14

I've had my fair share of people come in and out of my life. To some, I come off as the happy, outgoing, positive, bubbly 14 year old teenage girl. Deep down I'm a shy, scared, sealed, shut down 14 year old teenage girl. The only constant in my life is music. I can't go anywhere without it. I can see why I've had to depend on music. Being the middle child, I have been invisible. With the help of music, I was able to look at the world a different way and things became brighter and clearer. Before music, I had a hard time keeping my eyes on the prize. Reading is another way I'm able to escape my "invisibility".

Sitting in a room with music and a book is the way for me. It's also allowed me to avoid bad social situations. By keeping to myself, I have been able to avoid saying hurtful things, because when something is buried long enough, I will blow up. The idea of when I most like myself is when I'm by myself. Home is a place I can't be myself. My family always expects more than what I can give. Why does the middle child always get the stricter side of parents? I don't trust anyone anymore. When I have opened up, it's always come back to bite me. When I am asked "what's wrong" now I just tell them "I'm fine", even when I'm not.

Yet, I don't regret my life. My life is a new one, it's mine, and I love it.

BRYN, 14

Most of the things that I've been through make most people kill themselves. I'm not going to lie. It's pushed me to wanting to do that. But I decided I could make things better. By trying to be happy, my thought is that it would make people around me happy as well. I started to see a change in me realizing how good it feels to see someone you've made happy. My depression started at an early age. I remember feeling loneliness in kindergarten, which seems weird when I say I was depressed at six. I could choose to blame my mom for that, seeing she passed that depression down to me genetically. My teachers were concerned that I never played with anyone, never talked, and all I did was read books. It was through parent-teacher conferences that led to me being diagnosed in the second grade. They wanted to fill me up with pills for breakfast, lunch, and dinner. My parents wouldn't have it though. So my parents were upset about the diagnosis and I wasn't getting medicine for my depression, so I stopped eating. I skipped breakfast, and ate a salad with friends at lunch who were obsessed with their weight too. All this at eight years of age. My parents were confused and scared. So add an eating disorder to my already-diagnosed depression. I knew I would starve myself the rest of my life. I knew I would throw up everything I ate; that I would abuse laxatives and caffeine. And I knew I didn't care. I was first sent to an inpatient care center for two months. I got out early for good behavior but it was a lie, a scheme. I pretended to get better. I let them stuff me with bread, cereal, and bagels. I let them cover a wolf with sheep's clothing. I spent the next three years terrified of food and comforted myself with solitary action of being in my room while hunger pains persisted. I was hospitalized at the age of 11. I lost 40 pounds in 28 days. It amazed/scared my doctors and reveled at my so-called achievement. I felt superior, until I saw the look on my family's faces. My parents felt like failures. I went from 100 pounds to 60 pounds at five feet, five inches. I was also dehydrated and my brain was shrinking in certain places. Besides being on the verge of kidney failure, I had such infected ovaries that they had to be removed. Now I was in an inpatient center for three years. It was when I turned 12 that I decided I no longer wanted to live this way. I hated constantly being watched, but most of all, I was tired of doing this to myself. So after years of refusing antidepressants, I told my therapist it was time and that I wanted to be happy again. I owe a lot to my therapist for helping me. Together we focused on complimenting each other, learning how to love myself again. I found myself getting better mentally and physically. To see smiles on strangers' faces felt like the world was a better place. There are other "family dynamics" that compounded my personal issues I'd rather not get into other than to say I also experienced the foster care system, emotional, and physical abuse. I don't wish any of my experiences on anyone but I think I've grown into a better person because of it. I hope people see me as a happy, caring and go-with-the-flow type of person. I certainly strive to be perceived that way. All of my experiences have taught me perseverance, determination, and love. But perhaps the biggest thing it's shown me is that all of us are insignificantly significant.

JENNIFER, 13

When you're a kid, sometimes your imagination seems like the only thing you have. I know it to be false, but when you are eight years old you tend to exaggerate things. I imagined myself living on a huge farm with horses, cows, chickens, goats, and pigs. Growing up with a family of nine people on 2 ½ acres, my dream wasn't realistic. When I presented this idea to my mom she just laughed and told me "that's not happening girly." However, being a girl of high hopes, I kept the dream in the back of my head, hoping if it would ever be possible. Fast forward three years and my mom was on the phone with our neighbor who had every kind of animal imaginable. I was sitting on the couch, trying to pick up bits and pieces of what they were talking about. After my mom hung up I bombarded her with questions. We were getting five piglets from our neighbor! After four weeks of intense waiting, the day finally came when we got to take the piglets home. We ended up keeping one and naming him Hamlet. Each day we grew to love him more and more. He loved to sunbathe almost as much as he loved escaping into my dad's garden and ravaging it (to my dad's excitement [sarcasm]). Eventually we had to say goodbye, though not because we were going to eat him. My dad wasn't pleased about Hamlet's work on his garden. I was angry with my dad for a while but my mom told me to be grateful for the time I had with him. Having Hamlet made me look at things with a different outlook. I began to think about other things I cared about. I cared about my family and friends. I have come to realization that we can't control who or what stays in our lives and that all we can do is appreciate the time we have together because whatever you do or say could be your last on earth.

EVELYN, 14

It sounds cheesy but I have to give it up to my parents for being my inspiration to strive to be someone in this life. When I was little, I would try to copy my mom or help my dad whenever I could. I was raised to live by some golden rules: Try your best, take some risks, forgive, be kind, and love one another. These values have stuck with me my whole life. A situation at school reinforced how I knew I was on the right path. A girl I wasn't super close to approached me and trusted me to share some very deep stuff, and I was somehow able to help her through it. I realized for at least one person, I was caring and willing to lend a helping hand. As much negative garbage that exists in the school, I believe most of us don't like gossip and trash talk. We mostly value kindness. I may have a few friends that might not fully value and live by the same beliefs as me but I have always felt like I can be myself around them. I am proud of my ability to be authentic all the time.

CURTIS, 14

I am the youngest in my family. To me that is both a curse and a blessing. It's a blessing because I get what I want when I want. The curse is more of me watching my older siblings grow up without me. But it gave me the blueprints of what growing up was like and how high school would be. I can remember sitting on the floor playing with my toy cars and hearing my dad and brother argue and thinking I'm never going to be anything like that. It made me more aware of my feelings too. I could say I live a pretty normal life. I never had a traumatizing experience. I realize I'm pretty lucky to get this kind of life. I've heard so many stories of people who have never seen their dad or parents got divorced. The people around me is what's made me who I am. I've grown up to love comedy because I inherited my dad's sense of humor. My dad says I have a kind heart but no one can figure out where I got that trait. I have always seemed to care about other people. When I was six I saw a homeless person on the street and remember feeling bad. I have never wanted to cause pain to anyone and I don't like it when someone is hurt. I have also picked up the ability to know when someone is lying, probably because there were many times my dad said something but didn't keep his word on it. At my age the purpose of friends can be misunderstood. For me, the more I know a person, the more I like them as a friend. I don't care what their history is. Friends are not some group of people you pretend to be someone you're not, but people who you can open up to. I've learned the best value in being a good friend is the ability to listen. When a friend has something bad happen to him, I just listen. I only ever give my two cents when he ask me my opinion. <u>The Outsiders</u> book we read in class really spoke to me by saying that friends are like a family because they stick together no matter what.

ROURKE, 14

I cannot say that my life has been bad. I have heard about people who have had their parents break up, or a family member die, or a troubled past, but that hasn't happened to me. My life up until this point has been happy and filled with wonderful role models. I have a twin who has always been there for me despite having rough times in the past. My parents are strong hardworking people who have been happily married for almost twenty years. My family has always been supportive of my ideas and always push me to do my best. I do, however, have some uninspiring relatives. I have a druggy/homeless uncle, a crazy grandparent, and an uncle who had his first child by accident. Looking back now it seems like my family is the only normal group I am related to. My uncles on the other side of the family aren't too good either. One is jobless and the other is 19 and expecting a child. However, all these less-than-great people have shown me what not to be like as an adult so in a way I should be thanking them. They have been showing me what *not* to do ever since I was a kid. As a child I was influenced by science. To me it was the greatest thing in the world. I made it my duty to learn everything I could about everything there is. This led me down the path of particle physics, which to this day remains my favorite topic. In fifth grade I was already reading college level material on how the fundamentals of the universe functioned. Despite knowing all this, school has always been an issue with me. I would always get C's in elementary, and in junior high I couldn't make honor roll. This doesn't mean I am upset with my academics. In fact, I was nominated for a student of the year award. I try to be the best I can be every day, and I think that I have done a pretty good job so far. I have plenty of friends who have helped motivate me into becoming a better person. They influence me every day and help me strive for better and more advanced goals. I rarely thank these individuals for what they do, but hopefully they know how helpful they really are. One year ago I was struggling with serious confidence issues. I couldn't talk to people very openly and I lost most of the friends I had previously. I spent most of my free time sitting alone and working. Although this gave me a better grade and a place on the honor roll, it didn't give me anyone to talk to other than my brother. However, over the summer, my views changed from "it doesn't matter what I do" to "I can do whatever I want". I try not to think about the past very often. It's not that my past troubles me it's just that I know there could be a much better future. My view on life goes like this: Don't see the world as it is but as it should be. I have a hard time focusing and working only because I think that there are so many more influential things I could be doing. This is one of the reasons I don't like math. In the conditions I live in, math has become obsolete in my opinion. The internet and phones eliminate the need for math and I would rather spend my time designing or filming. My life has always been a good one. I strive to be better in every situation physically or emotionally. This doesn't mean I am not happy with things. I just know that I could be happier. I enjoy filming, acting, performing, building, improv/comedy, or anything else that exercises my mind and body. I truly believe if people everywhere (especially teenagers) could just smile a little more, to me, that would change the world.

CELINE, 14

I would say I have a very good life with loving parents. My parents have raised me into a great person. They have taught me to be kind and respectful to others, and the importance responsibility at school and everyday life. But, sometimes I wish they would just trust me. I know I have made mistakes like most kids do, but I've learned from them. If only they could trust me with my friends. I am glad I have them because they give me such great advice when it comes to school. Over the year, I have realized who my true and fake friends are. I'm very thankful for the ones who have stayed by side, for they always find a way to cheer me up. I used to think that friends were just the ones you laugh with and talk to. But it's much more than that. They are the ones that touch your hearts. They're the people that can make you smile, can share your secrets with, cry with, make memories, and just have fun. I have learned that it doesn't matter how popular you are or how many friends you have. As long as you be yourself, you shouldn't care what people think. The only thing that matters is that you are happy with who you are. If there's one piece of advice I can pass along, it's don't change so people will like you. You don't need to impress anyone. Just being yourself will attract people who like the real you. I realized that not everyone is going to like you and that's okay. Not everyone is the same and likes the same things. When you pretend to be someone you're not they call you fake but when you are yourself, people still judge you for the real you. True friends will love you for who you are. Middle school will always have drama. There will always be those judgmental kids. Just block out the negativity. If you replace negative thoughts with positive thoughts you can achieve great things. If you believe in yourself you can reach your goals and set many more to reach. Just put your mind to it and you will be able to accomplish them.

KEEVA, 14

While growing up, my parents continuously gave me structure, taught me respect, manners, and discipline. At the age of four my family moved to the suburbs. Shortly after moving we purchased an ex-racehorse to call ours. From then on, my mom and I rescued horses that were starving, near death, suffering from injuries, or neglected. One horse we rescued even dug her own grave and could be seen laying in the holes she dug. This has helped shape me, along with the fact that I'm an only child. So who gets all the chores and responsibilities? Me. Both my parents work, and from the ages of 6-10 I would get off the bus and enter an empty house. And when my dad did come home he would get drunk and make rude remarks to me about my weight or something else. My mom got tired of the bickering and filed for divorce. Again, being an only child, I was left to my own self and thoughts. I learned to stand back and observe, which always comes in handy. I started gaining weight after my parents' divorce. I started getting harassed at school, and then my grandfather (dad's dad) died from 40 years of drinking whiskey. It kinda shaped my dad into reality. The divorce papers were dropped after he stopped drinking and smoking, and leaving more time and money for the family. While things at home started straightening out, I continued to get bullied at school until I lost weight and cleaned myself up. Since I've grown up so lonely, I've always been an independent, hard worker along with always saying "please" and "thank you" (thanks mom). Even though there were a series of events that hardened me at a young age I am proud to be who I am in school. I now know being myself and surrounding myself with true friends not only makes me happier, but gives me more opportunities.

ARTIE, 14

I believe what makes me who I am is that I come from a strong and supportive family. I don't worry about what other people think. Dating is not a big concern for me, because it could be an unnecessary emotional stress that I am not interested in. Also I don't get involved in other people's business, because it is not my concern and I respect their privacy. I think this way because my main concerns are my family, myself, and my education. I don't worry about girlfriends or how I dress because it doesn't matter to me. I care mostly about my family because when you're in a pickle they're the people you can always count on the most. No matter what situation you find yourself in, they have your back. They are always there to help you out when you're on a streak of bad luck. I care about my education because I want to get into a good college to help me get a job. I want to be able support myself, live comfortably, still have enough money to have fun, and possibly support a family at some point.

I care about myself. I know this sounds cheesy but you only get one chance at life and I don't want to make a poor decision and end it early because of a dumb disease or stupid mistake. There are still too many things I want to do.

I am who I am because of my parents, teachers, and good friends. They helped me learn right from wrong, how to be a good student, how to choose my friends by their actions and not their appearance. Most importantly they taught me how to be myself.

RHONA, 13

I'm an eighth grader. I'm on the honor roll and I'm planning on starting freshman year off with advanced classes, and I hope I can continue with advanced classes throughout high school. I've played the violin since I was six and I'm in two orchestras, one of which I'm a concert master. I spend time with my friends, like all other teenagers. We hang out on the weekends because we all have some kind of practice after school. Then to round off my personality, I run track. I run the mile, the 800 meter (half mile) and the 4x400 meter relay. This is the first year I've done track, or any sport, and I made it to the championships. I'm the best miler on the team and the second best 800 runner. I don't think there's one specific event that made me do well in school, hang out with certain people, or run track. But there is one day that pushed me towards violin.

When I was six years old I got my first violin for Christmas. It was too big and the bow was pretty bad but I loved it. My parents got it for me because I had been begging them to let me play for about a year. That's thanks to my grandma on my dad's side. My grandma loves classical music. She plays it in the car and on her little CD player in her living room. I think all she wanted was someone in the family who loved classical music as much as she did. My brother was obviously a no go on classical music and my cousin was too immature and impatient to really stop and listen to something without lyrics. She had faith in me though. She took me to this strings festival in Oregon, where she lives. I listened to people perform from soloists all the way to symphonies. Throughout the show, there were musicians who stood on the other side of the festival area and let kids try out the instruments. They taught us how to hold it and the strings they had. When it was my turn, I impressed the musicians with my knowledge that I had from my grandma. But when I tried the violin, I knew I wanted to do that for the rest of my life. So I guess eight years, four different orchestras and hours of practice has made me a pretty good violinist.

I remember my first day of kindergarten. I was wanting to find a way to impress my teacher so she would like me during the year. So during the summer I picked up my first chapter book. It was the series with the two girls who are best friends and they can turn into fairies so they can defeat Jack Frost and his goblins. Each book came with a charm for the bracelet that came with the first book in the series. I finished that first book on my first day of kindergarten and proudly walked up to my teacher and said, "Look Mrs. Smith, I finished my first chapter book." That's right. I was teacher's pet from day one. It's my parents' fault. Ever since I could open my eyes, my parents read to me before bed every night. When I learned to read, I read to them. And now, ten years later, I still read before bed every night. In fourth grade, I read a ninth grade level book. In eighth grade, I read at a college level. My grandma on my mom's side is the reason I'm good at math. I would spend weekends at my grandma on my dad's side baking cookies and learning to swim. My grandma on my mom's side was a little different. Instead of swimming races, she would have my brother and me see who could solve ten multiplication problems the fastest. By fourth grade, I was doing eighth grade math. In eighth grade, I'm doing eleventh grade math. Now, I wasn't good at everything growing up. School and music and going to my friends' house was my life, and that's fine. But athletics was not my thing.

My brother played lots of sports. He's played baseball, football, basketball, and wrestling. I played violin. I couldn't run like Aiden. I couldn't throw like Aiden. And I definitely could not catch like Aiden. None of my friends cared. I had two athletic friends with one friend, Chelsea, just like me. She wore these colorful, fuzzy pants with tails and she loved beavers. I never called Chelsea my best friend. I spent more time with my best friend and I knew her longer. But I told Chelsea everything. The things I just couldn't tell my best friend. In the fourth grade my group of friends welcomed someone new to our group. He was smart and athletic (for a fourth grader). But he never liked Chelsea and me. We were both smart but we weren't athletic. He teased us for a lot of things but the thing I remember most is when he made fun of the way I ran. I used to dance but I wasn't good so I quit. I wasn't good because I never knew where my arms and legs were exactly. I knew where they were supposed to be, but not where they were. This showed when I ran. I never got very far on our cardio tests in P.E. because I spent so much energy flailing my disproportionate limbs everywhere. And I could never keep up with my friends. I don't think the things our new "friend" said to me was what made me feel bad about my athletic abilities. It was when my best friend didn't tell him to shut up. But Chelsea did. I still don't know why I never called her my best friend. After fourth grade, Chelsea moved to England. I see her once a year when they come visit and they're moving back this summer. But fifth and sixth grade without here, without someone to tell him to shut up, weren't fun. It still wasn't what he said. It was when Chelsea stuck up for me, I knew someone cared. When my "best friend" didn't say a word, or sometimes laughed is when it started getting to me. So, I did a dumb thing that turned out to be a good thing. I changed to make him shut up. In seventh grade, I started running after school on the treadmill every day. It was the little victories that counted. The first time I ran a half mile at a ten-minute mile pace, I was happy. The first time I ran a ten-minute mile, or when I finally made it over that super steep hill by the driving range without stopping I was proud. After about a year of training on my own, I joined the track team. I chose the two longest events and part way through the third meet the coaches told me I was running another event - the third longest event. The first race I ever ran was the mile against Fairview Middle School. I was so nervous, I almost cried. The night before I went over the checklist of things that I needed so many times my brother had it memorized. The most intense part of every race is when the official says "runners take your marks" and we all step up to our line and wait for the gun to go off. At the end of the first lap, I was in last. The rest is kind of a blur of people in orange jerseys and people in blue jerseys but coming around the last corner of the last lap, I was in second. I moved to lane two and went into a full sprint, hoping my kick was faster than the opponent's girl. It was, and I ran right passed her and finished first. I placed in every event at every meet except at league championships. I came in 13th out of the top 16 girls from 14 schools. After finishing the mile in six minutes, seven seconds I was remembering back to that kid who made fun of the way my legs kicked out when I ran. Who needs someone to tell him to shut up when four years later I can show him up?

I guess my life and personality doesn't always change with just one moment of one day. And even though we say we don't, I think at some point, everyone changes themselves to meet someone's expectations. But sometimes we get lucky, and we change and find that we changed into exactly who we were meant to be. I know a lot of people who are fake in junior high. I try not to be, and I know most people do too. But my love for music and reading, my knack for math, the freedom of running into the wind, right past your opponent, and most of all, true best friends, that's never fake.

TEAGUE, 14

I tend to think I made myself who I am by learning from my own mistakes and my family's. I am always trying to make myself the best I can be, the best student, the best leader, the best kid in the family.

I watch my brother and sister make mistakes and I always think about how I wouldn't make the same mistakes they have made. I've seen both my siblings talk back to my parents and I've seen the consequences. I don't like making my parents mad. People always tell me I'm kind of like a small version of my dad and I wouldn't argue that. He is an old school kind of guy, listens to older music, enjoys watching sports, and always tells stories of the old days.

Camping is a family tradition and I love sitting in front of the fire and looking up at the stars. It gives me the chance to think not just about my life but others as well. I always try and help others into improving their lives. To me I'm always thinking selflessly but sometimes forget to act that way. I also credit TV shows for helping me make better choices. I've used mistakes from the characters and tell myself I will never make that same mistake. Yet I sometimes will slip up and make them. I guess I could say I am trying to make myself the best possible. This past year I've been more focused on becoming better at being the person I imagine myself to be. Before, I would think about the day and realize I was acting fake. Today, I'm satisfied with who I am and what I'm doing. I've made better choices with what I do and with who I'm doing that with. I'm glad my family has given me the experiences and great moments in my life.

KARLY, 13

I believe that the person we become is directly related to the experiences we have and the people we interact with, both in positive and negative ways. I've always been a shy person, always wanted the same career, always have been the same person. Doing things, even the simplest things, are difficult for me if they involve other people. I always try my best in school. I'm a perfectionist and I probably would be diagnosed with Obsessive Compulsive Disorder. I believe that my perfectionism is in my blood because I've always wanted to do my best and I don't enjoy doing activities that I don't excel. This trait has helped me become a very strong student and it will enable me to realize my dream of becoming a veterinarian. My perfectionism is no picnic though. I put a lot of pressure on myself to be perfect. I was put to the test when I recently had surgery. My surgeon said I would miss six weeks of school but I was determined to get back to school much sooner. I pushed myself to get to school even though I was in constant pain and often in a fog because of my pain medication. I was in a wheelchair and then crutches for months, so I had to rely on other people to help me. I struggled as a student, for the medication made it very difficult to focus. My confidence with learning is still recovering from this event. It was very scary sitting in class and not comprehending what was going on around me.

My teachers have always had a positive effect on me, but after the surgery I saw how truly understanding and encouraging they are. They supported me when I needed extra time or instruction due to my medical condition. I was lucky to have great role models as teachers who made sure I had a positive classroom environment and they reinforced their belief in me and the potential I have to achieve any goal I set. Through this I learned to believe that of myself too. When I look at who I am, I believe my identity is measured by my academic success and what kind of friend I am to others. I always try my best and I am a loyal friend. This makes me content.

KLAY, 13

My family has supported me in everything that I do. They always have my back and I can always rely on them to be there for me when I need them. Even though we can get in arguments and fight sometimes, I know that they will always love me no matter what I do. Having a family that is so amazing makes me want to be like them. I want to be able to have a supportive role in other people's lives.

Whenever my grandma was diagnosed with cancer, I realized I was definitely not the person I was the day before. That type of news happens to other people every day. I quickly learned to live every second with people to the fullest, and not take for granted the good times. Most important, always say "I love you" to your family before hanging up the phone or going to bed.

My dad is from Romania, which is one of Europe's poorest countries. He grew up in a really sad situation, with negative degree weather and no winter clothes. Food and water was also hard to come by. Ever since I was born, my family has gone on missions trips with my church to help feed the poor people in the villages in Romania. When I was nine years old, we were on our way up the mountains to feed this really poor village. When we arrived I experienced something that I will never forget. I saw whole families living in mud huts with no clothes, food, or water. It looked like something you see in in apocalyptic movies. While we were feeding these people, they were overwhelmed with happiness. When they saw us with the food, water and other basic living needs, they were crying out of pure joy. Seeing the kids' faces when we were helping them out made me think how much we take these things for granted in life. We get so worked up when we have our phones to look at social media or even when our parents cook what we don't like for dinner. We (kids) don't realize there are people on the other side of the world who have absolutely nothing except themselves or their family. I try never to complain over the smallest things because of the things I have seen.

CHRISTIANA, 14

I've always been a quiet, laid back, go-with-the-flow kind of gal. I've never been outgoing, spontaneous, or a seeker of attention. When I was younger I always felt lesser than my family—a major inconvenience. I was made fun of often and felt very alone. It didn't help when my sister was diagnosed with a couple of diseases that I'd feel more alone. Things revolved around her and making sure she was okay. I just kept to myself and stayed in my room with my music. You would think things would change as I battle through adolescence, but they haven't. Between the countless arguments over freedom or grades amidst my sister and my parents, I simply prefer being alone. My mom calls me an over-observer and over-thinker. I do contemplate everything, which can cause problems. While I feel independent, I also find myself being an inconvenience due to my "unneeded presence". There is a voice in my head that always says "Christiana, you're unwanted, and the cause of so many problems. Stop screwing things up." As for my friends, it's weird that they're my friends seeing they are complete opposite of me. Most of them are loud, and obnoxious. They try to get me to be rowdy and sociable, and it works sometimes. But then I feel fake because I have to force myself to be loud, fun and upbeat when I am with them. The reality is I'd rather be alone in my room with a good book and music. I think if I changed my friends to people I shared common interests with I'd be a lot happier, and probably more self-confident. But when I surround myself around people who find my interests boring, I don't want to be labeled as "dull", so I stick to being uncomfortable and unhappy at the expense of not being disliked. I think everyone has multiple sides to them. I think everyone has a fun loving, rebellious side, yet a soft and sweet side too. Unfortunately for most of us, people don't see our true selves. It's a shame actually. If everyone saw the reason and purpose behind the way we do things, people might be actually less judgmental and accept people for who they are. That would be truly beautiful. We need to try that for a change. Imagine if everyone could see how happy we could make ourselves and other people.

www.ingramcontent.com/pod-product-compliance
Lightning Source LLC
Chambersburg PA
CBHW071626080526
44588CB00010B/1292